Reckoning with Aggression

RECKONING WITH
AGGRESSION

Theology, Violence, and Vitality

Kathleen J. Greider

Westminster John Knox Press
Louisville, Kentucky

Except where noted, scripture quotations from the New Revised Standard Version
of the Bible are copyright © 1989 by the Division of Christian Education
of the National Council of the Churches of Christ in the U.S.A.
and are used by permission.

Grateful acknowlegment is made to the following copyright holders for permission
to reprint excerpts from *Through the Eyes of Women: Insights for Pastoral Care*, ed.
Jeanne Stevenson Moessner, copyright © 1996 Augsburg Fortress and excerpts
from Kathleen J. Greider, "Reckoning with Aggression: Invesigations in Violence
and Vitality, *Journal of Pastoral Theology* 6 (June 1996): 37–54.

Book design by Jennifer K. Cox
Cover design by Alec Bartsch

First edition
Published by Westminster John Knox Press
Louisville, Kentucky

This book is printed on acid-free paper that meets
the American National Standards Institute Z39.48 standard. ♾

PRINTED IN THE UNITED STATES OF AMERICA
97 98 99 00 01 02 03 04 05 06 — 10 9 8 7 6 5 4 3 2 1

Library of Congress Cataloging-in-Publication Data

Greider, Kathleen J., date.
  Reckoning with aggression : theology, violence, and vitality /
Kathleen J. Greider. — 1st ed.
      p.   cm.
  Includes bibliographical references and index.
  ISBN 0-664-25668-6
  1. Aggressiveness (Psychology)—Religious aspects—Christianity.
I. Title.
BT736.15.G74   1997
241′.697—dc21   97-14696

Contents

Acknowledgments

I AM GRATEFUL for colleagues who, through reading and response, have supported, critiqued, and enriched this book: Ann Belford Ulanov, my primary mentor; Russell H. Davis; Carter Heyward; Harry Wells Fogarty; William M. Clements; Timothy G. Staveteig; Mary Elizabeth Moore; Frank Rogers, Jr.; Ann Taves; Carroll Saussy; and Lee H. Butler, Jr.

I am grateful for my colleagues and students at the Claremont School of Theology: my faculty colleagues who, with their love of scholarship and collaborative spirit, create a facilitating environment for writing; my dean, Marjorie Suchocki, and the Board of Trustees, for their support of my sabbatical leave during 1994–1995; my students, for teaching me a great deal about constructive aggressiveness; Olga Morales, faculty secretary, and Louise Graves and Kristen Leslie, my research assistants during the writing of this book, for their skill and good humor.

I am grateful for the persons whom I have had the privilege of offering pastoral care, counseling, and psychotherapy. Several have generously given me permission to try to describe their experience, and all have honored and taught me about aggression by inviting me into their struggles.

I am grateful for my colleagues in several professional societies and for the immense benefits I gained through discussion of these ideas with them: the Society for Pastoral Theology; the Person, Culture, and Religion Group of the American Academy of Religion; and the International Pastoral Care Network for Social Responsibility.

I am grateful for colleague-friends who read *me* at critical moments: Kathy Black; Karen Baker-Fletcher; Lori Anne Ferrell; Brita Gill-Austern; Anne Gilson; Ellie Maher; Joretta Marshall; Diane Moore; Nancy Ramsay; Chris Smith; Daryl Smith; and Glenda Walther. I am also grateful for Pat Brooks, who enabled me to have a place in the mountains for writing.

I am grateful for my friends and family who, without exception, tolerated my long silences and absences with care and patience. My love and thanks to my family, especially, Jane, Berneda, Harold, Susan, Doris, Mike, Sue, Tom, Kris, Bill, Diane, Mel, Pat, Mina, Mabel, Emily, Kelsey, Ben, David, and Derek.

I am grateful for Jane Heckles: her prodding love, unfailing confidence, and gentle example are daily wonders. Because these qualities also helped me to get constructively aggressive enough to write this book, it is dedicated to her.

Introduction

Now the earth was . . . filled with violence . . . for all flesh had corrupted its ways upon the earth. And God said to Noah, "I have determined to make an end of all flesh. . . ."
—Genesis 6:11–13

Complexity has resulted in a failure of nerve.
—Sharon D. Welch,
A Feminist Ethic of Risk

God did not give us a spirit of timidity, but a spirit of power and love and self-control.
—2 Timothy 1:7, RSV

Origins of This Study of Aggression

I AM MOTIVATED in this study of aggression by two primary assumptions. First, decrying violence and devising solutions to it are nearly pointless unless at least equal attention is given to helping individuals and communities cultivate the tremendous vitality required to live ethically and empathically and thereby decrease violence. Paradoxically, prescriptions issued for the misuse of human power are effective only if we learn how to marshal constructively the human power required to actually carry them out. Otherwise our hopes and designs for nonviolence do little more than hang like albatross around our necks, increasing our immobility, our feelings of powerlessness and guilt, and our yearning for a divine rescue.

Second, though it is easily overlooked, I assume there is meaning and value in the ambiguity and relationality imputed to aggression in common discourse. Often English-speakers decry aggression as violence. Not infrequently, however, our descriptions of aggressiveness characterize it as a vital aspect of the constructive power required to defend ourselves and our loved ones and to come together collaboratively in community. Sometimes aggressiveness seems to provide us with the backbone to stand up to violence and do right by one another. Interestingly, social-scientific studies of aggression ignore (and sometimes disdain) this complex popular connotation; scholars focus with near-uniformity on the role of aggression in violence.

I am curious, however, about the ambiguity and relationality we seem to experience relative to aggression. How can we understand these allusions and testimonies to aggression's mixed values and to its role in both alienation and alliance? What might be the value and risks of such a conceptualization? In this book I argue the paradox that we need vitality of aggression to decrease violent aggressiveness and that a new formulation of aggression in theology and spiritual practice, one attentive to ambiguity and relationality in aggression, will increase our capacity to shape aggressive expressions that resist violence and are life-affirming and just.

The problems of violence and vitality are as persistent in human history as the tides and were awakened in me when I was a girl. A multitude of questions flow from the problem of violence. Why are human beings violent? Which is more violent, murder or poverty? Why do we use our power to push the less powerful to the margins, often in the name of religion or other cherished values? What do we accomplish when we assault—or, more subtly, insult—others' bodies and spirits? Why do we torment ourselves? How can we navigate the complex field of violence's values, where inflicting injury usually is wrong but, under some rationales—self-defense, discipline, governmental austerity, theological orthodoxy—doing harm is claimed to be necessary or even right? Since people lash out at strangers who have done them no harm and are cruel to those they love, on what basis can we hope for the end of violence? Have we, like our ancestors described in the story of Noah, corrupted the earth and ourselves again? Or is our condition much worse? Are we toxic with violence, beyond redemption even if we hole ourselves up two by two?

Granted, I was too serious as a child. But children and teenagers are more attuned to violence than some adults want to admit, seeing it in their homes, schools, and religious communities at least as often as through the much-maligned media. While growing up, I knew people who inflicted suffering—physically and emotionally, systemically and privately—on each other and themselves, most often right alongside being loving and decent. Not only did other people's violence terrify me, but my own frustrations and fears also brought to consciousness violent impulses and lapses within myself. When I was barely a teenager, I began to realize how profoundly violence is gendered. I knew violent men and violent women, but the form and impact of their acts of violence were usually quite different. As a white child growing into adulthood in the midst of racial segregation, it took longer for me to become aware of how violence is racialized in soul-searing racism. However, putting it all together over the years, the extent to which human beings experience and inflict violence still haunts me.

More questions—less often discussed, but arguably more important—flow from the problem of vitality or, more precisely, its elusiveness. When our enthusiasm seems exhausted by work or trouble, where can we find, personally and collectively, the vigor to tackle and outlast life's sufferings, to live out and live up to what we say we believe? If money and power are elixirs, why are the poor not infrequently dynamic in spirit, while privileged people are often bereft of soul and deadened? Where has vitality gone for the many people whose life energies drain away into pits of depression and anomie, leaving them excruciatingly disempowered and demoralized? If we are religious and think of ourselves as made in the image of God, why are we reflections of sacred power even less frequently than we are reflections of sacred love?

Questions about vitality and violence are interwoven. Why are human beings so often without vitality consistent, capable, and constructive enough to oppose violence and sustain a nonviolent passion? Which is more likely to further violence, too much passion or too little? At the merest sign of disagreement, some groups and individuals go numb or flee. What are the costs when conflict is held off by diffuseness of identity or avoidance? Given the mandate for freedom at the core of most of our religions—and souls—how do enslaved people, and their supporters, tolerate even one moment of oppression? Where can we find the integrity and, more basically, the grit to control our own propensity to do harm, and that of our communities? What can enable us to face the complexity of modern, faithful living and fight what feminist theologian Sharon Welch calls our "failure of nerve"?

Influenced by the quiet determination of Amish culture, peaceful but resolute living was the norm in the rural and deeply religious milieu of Lancaster County, Pennsylvania, where I grew up. My family and I were struggling tenant farmers in that region beloved for one-day barn raisings and plowing "by hand." Farm life required of women, children, and men bold risks, strong bodies, and endless labor. Underneath our typically restrained Germanic demeanors lay a passion of sorts for toughness and resilience. The demands of the land paled in comparison to the demands of the faith. In Sunday services and regular camp meetings, preachers called us to a faith hard-y enough to withstand temptation and heart-y enough to extend compassion.

There were so many times, and still are, however, when I hungered for more zest, more spontaneity, and, especially, more courage in myself and in my community—the kind of God-given spirit described by the writer of the second letter to Timothy, "not . . . a spirit of timidity, but a spirit of power and love and self-control" (1:7, RSV). As the demands of adulthood loomed, it seemed to me that my people were too often stiflingly contained, excessively cautious, dispassionately agreeable, and lukewarm. Timidity was attributed to femininity, and so girls and women especially were expected to live in a circumspect way—not to draw attention to ourselves, take up too much space, have strong opinions, initiate decisive action, or gather resources for ourselves. It took longer for me to become aware of the risks taken by others who, though banned from society's center, still dared to live boldly and unapologetically.

Both violence and vitality have to do with human agency, and on that subject traditional Christian doctrine seems to give with one hand and take away with the other. The Protestant evangelical church in which I was reared called its followers to vital, powerful living—put your light on a stand, go the second mile, save the perishing, free the captives, and feed the hungry. However, in the church of my childhood, as in many Christian communities, the faithful are usually left on their own to figure out—if they do at all—how to rally constructively the tremendous power necessary to walk a path like the one chosen by Jesus of Nazareth. Instead, churches typically occupy themselves with all the ways humans use their power to sin. Unintentionally, perhaps, they shape individuals and congregations too often suspicious, afraid, or ashamed of their own power.

I also struggled with the contradictions between our religious declarations about the sinfulness of violence, religiously inspired violence, and failures of religious peoples to outwit or sometimes even stand up to violence. Paraphrasing one of the old hymns we sang, our dreams and deeds were—are—not one but "always two."[1] As I awakened to the demands of work, belief, and love and to the violent and unjust subjugation of human vitality, my search grew more urgent for the strength to make my dreams and my deeds more nearly one.

These questions about violence, vitality, and their interrelationship in the just and unjust use of human power fundamentally motivate my interest in aggression. Put most simply: Is it possible to find or create among us a power finely tuned enough to destroy what needs to be destroyed—the structures of violence and other evils—without destroying each other? Is it possible to find or craft among us a power finely tuned enough to construct what begs to be constructed—personal and communal lives of passion, justice, gusto, and even abandon—without constructing violence, without harming one another and ourselves?

I address some of these questions in subsequent chapters, though, of course, I do not and cannot offer answers for all of them. As a scholar, I am wary of admitting that these questions are my deep, original starting point, for they are huge and unwieldy, like the questions of childhood. Adults know they cannot be answered, at least not in full or finally. Yet, despite academic rigor and sophistication, they remain among the most frequent and difficult questions I confront every day as a scholar and teacher, as a pastor and counselor, and as a human being.

Why Aggression?

Until several years ago, I paid little attention to popular references to aggression's ambiguity and relationality. My rudimentary understanding of scholarship on human aggression—biology, social sciences, ethics—had led me to think of aggression as being the same as violence, or nearly so. Though there are obvious interpersonal ramifications, I was taught that aggressiveness is primarily a personal trait and is studied through the observation of physically violent individual behavior. Some attention was given in the literature to the study of the social context of the individual's aggressive behavior, but aggressive persons and groups and the emergence of aggression between (as compared to within) people got little mention. There was virtually nothing in my religious and theological education to cause me to question these approaches to aggression. Aggression was equated with sin, or nearly so.

Then I discovered depth psychological writings on aggression. As I studied the works of those who explore the often unconscious and complex dynamics of the psyche and relationship, especially the work of British pediatrician and psychoanalyst Donald Woods Winnicott, a different view of aggression began to emerge. Many of the claims in this literature ran contrary to what I had been taught was true about aggression, but I could not argue that these ideas ran counter to my experience. I was intrigued with the descriptions of our aggression's ambiguity—its capacity to do good as well as harm, and of the close relationship between aggression and love. Just as important and perhaps even more novel was the discussion of aggression as both an individual trait and a relational phenomenon; aggression happens within and between persons and groups. Perhaps most tantalizing was the claim that both violence and lack of vitality are problems of aggression.

As I began to investigate this view of aggression, I found fainter but similar suggestions in some feminist and nonviolence theory and in liberation theologies. These sources suggested that the meaning and interpretation of aggressive behavior is influenced by race, gender, and class. I began to think that a hermeneutic of suspicion needed to be applied to aggression. Why is aggression generally characterized as undesirable and widely denied to subjugated classes, but its energies and powers often enjoyed and abused by dominant classes?

These views confronted me with my psychospiritual distance from my own aggression, especially regarding my life as a woman and a person of faith, socialized in both identities to be unaggressive. They awakened my concern about the personal and social causes and consequences—especially the losses—of human denial and demonizing of aggression. Though the implications were rarely developed, in such a view of aggression there were exciting intimations for both religious and social life and thought.

This book explores aggression as one partial but potentially effective response to problems of violence and vitality. My hope is that these views of aggression create a bridge onto which we can draw our powers to harm and to help, toward the transformation of both. Reckoning with aggression's complexity might yield a key to the ambiguity and relationality of power.

Reckoning with Aggression

In this book, I argue a two-part thesis. First, human aggression has been distorted into extremes of violence and passivity, or lack of vitality, largely by neglect of aggression's ambiguity and relationality. In short, aggression is in dire need of repair. Second, reckoning with aggression—especially with aggression's ambiguity and relationality—can both decrease violence and increase vitality and justice. Aggression can be repaired and reparative. "Reckoning with" aggression requires deep and wide-ranging reflection on aggression's costs and values, disciplined efforts to develop more relationship to aggression in oneself and in others, and care-filled, ethical utilization of aggression.

I develop this thesis in five chapters. In chapter 1, I argue that aggression is a crucial topic for study because our experience and knowledge about aggression is problem-ridden and because aggression has been identified, but not much developed, as a potential resource for vital, effective living. In chapter 2, I use Winnicott's work, supplemented with other approaches, to construct a comprehensive psychosocial and relational view of aggression's origins and meanings. My goal is to offer a picture of aggression detailed enough to represent its complexity but manageable enough to serve as a guide for reflection and praxis for those who are not specialists in aggression theory. Chapter 3 offers some foundational observations for a constructive theology of aggression. Aggression has only rarely been the explicit topic of theological discussion. Yet, as I argue here, aggression has often been a subtext in theology and has significance for theological reflection and for religious and spiritual life.

The two final chapters extend the discussion more explicitly into praxis. In these chapters I attempt to show—less theoretically and more concretely— what it means to "reckon with" aggression in light of its ambiguity and relationality. For the sake of introduction, thus far I have been talking about aggression as if it has universal meaning. But we must not go far into our discussion before acknowledging that aggression has vastly different meanings in different cultural contexts.[2] Thus, in chapter 4 I explore what the cultures of gender and race reveal about aggression's ambiguity and relationality. In chapter 5, I examine some issues raised by aggression in spiritual life and in the practice of pastoral care and counseling.

Because space does not permit a full discussion of method, brief description must suffice. To accomplish the tasks just named, I use a method I call "critical collaboration" to construct a feminist pastoral theological approach to the issue of aggression. In this book, I seek to bring feminist, pastoral, and theological perspectives into critical collaboration, which is a process of inter-weaving distinct disciplinary approaches and insights so as to correct, support, and expand the knowledge available to us about aggression from any one of these disciplines. Critical collaboration is one way of accomplishing the multi-disciplinary work that is inherent to pastoral theology.

My approach in this book is feminist in that I use feminist theory and study of the diversity of women's lives as a particular window into human need, the vast structures of systemic and private oppressions that hinder fullness of life, and experiences of aggression. The reality of oppression results in feminism's close attention to issues of power, the application of a hermeneutic of suspicion to proscriptions from dominant persons or groups about the nature of ethical and moral behavior, and empowerment and liberation of those who are marginal-ized.[3] My approach is theological in that, through this study of aggression, I am seeking to extend a bit our understanding of God, the sacred power that imparts life, value, meaning, and purpose to all aspects of the creation. Because of my own interests and training, my theological method is often theological anthro-pology—reflections on human nature and life, including our suffering and heal-ing, and our efforts to construct ethical frameworks. My approach is pastoral in that I seek to offer multidisciplinary theory and method that best support clergy, laypeople, and other seekers in the development and sustenance of personal and communal lives characterized by mutual empowerment, liberation from evil,[4] health, and spiritual depth. In this book, I try to show that pastoral method es-tablishes and nurtures an interplay between theory and lived life, where religious reflection comes out of and is tested by concrete experience, and vice versa.[5]

I have several overlapping audiences in mind as I write. Perhaps the most diverse audience for this book consists of individuals and groups, whether scholars or general readers, who struggle with the complex issues of power and aggression in the church and other settings; this book is written for any-one who has ever misused their aggression and for anyone who has ever felt they needed to be more aggressive. Since childhood is such a formative and formidable arena for aggression, I include significant resources for parents and all other adults who are responsible for children's well-being and maturation—for example, extended family, religious educators and other teachers, and pas-tors. Though I use primarily Christian theological perspectives, since that is my tradition and training, I try to write from a nonsectarian point of view for reli-gious and spiritual seekers in search of some help with the intersection of re-ligion, spirit, and aggression. Additionally, I am writing for women and men interested in liberation movements—gender studies, racial justice, gay and les-bian rights, and others—in that a spectrum of aggressiveness is essential and controversial in strategizing and carrying out social change. I am writing as well for those who work and teach in ministry and counseling, where practitioners struggle with the multivalency of human aggressiveness in congregational and therapeutic settings.

The impressions of aggression and aggression research that I record here are shaped profoundly by my own cultural context, which is one reason I have offered some description of it in this introduction. My many identities— being female, Euro-American of German and Scottish descent, a Christian pastor and pastoral psychotherapist, a citizen of the United States, closely affiliated with religious organizations—are among the factors that both deepen and narrow my ability to observe and reflect on aggression. I am most equipped to address dynamics of aggression in my own cultural contexts and in the intersection between my own and other cultures, though I hope that persons in other cultural locations will respond to and benefit from this work. While my purpose in this book is not to construct a multicultural study of aggression, I do attempt to provide an intercultural study that reflects on how the meanings and values of aggression shift as they are encountered in areas of cultural overlap.

Social location imparts another level of complexity to my authority to undertake this project. For a woman to be writing about aggression's values as well as its costs may seem strange in light of the fact that women are so often targets of violent aggressiveness, and in light of prevalent beliefs that women are not as aggressive as men or, at least, are not to behave as though they are. Yet, as a respondent to my work has noted, a man might be considered without authority to write a book that explores the possibility that aggression might have positive potential, precisely because of the extent of male violence against women. Then again, as a white person living in racist United States, I may have no more credibility than a man to write about aggression's positive potential, since violent aggressiveness by white people has done so much harm to people of color in this country and around the world. In all these ways, trying to communicate, collaborate, or merely live together peacefully amid cultural diversity is made difficult in large part because of aggression.

The Terminological Terrain

Issues of definition are complicated and controversial in the study of aggression, and I touch on this topic throughout the book. At this point it is important only to state my working definitions of terms central to this study. For reasons I detail later, I depart from definitions of aggression that focus exclusively on its relationship to harm-causing behavior. I base this work on a broader understanding, where *aggression* is significant energy, vigor, agency, enterprise, boldness, and resilience. This foundational meaning of aggression in the English language is suggested by its etymology: *aggression* comes from the Latin *aggredi,* to go forward, to approach.[6] Aggression frequently has about it qualities of immediacy and embodiment, either literal or metaphorical. Aggression is a form of power and, like power, carries the potential of both positive and negative effects. Aggression manifests in a gamut of feeling-thoughts, behaviors, and qualities: initiative, motivation, proficiency, assertion, competition, conflict, confrontation, anger, rage, militancy, war.[7] Because *aggression* carries such a wide range of meanings among English-speakers, I use appropriate qualifiers when I speak of aggression's specifically negative or positive aspects. When I speak of aggression or its manifestations without qualification, I am referencing aggression's simultaneous personal and social dimensions and evoking aggression's multivalency. Further, it is a central tenet of this study that aggression is not something outside our control, and to remind us of that, I speak frequently of "our" aggression or "human" aggression.

Violence is force against persons, objects, or principles that intentionally or unintentionally injures, damages, or destroys. Feminist process theologian Marjorie Suchocki puts it succinctly: "Violence has many forms existing along a continuum from obvious to subtle, but at its base, violence is the destruction of well-being."[8] By use of the word *vitality,* I refer to essential aliveness and life-affirmation, to human agency that manifests in passion and capacity to endure.

What does it mean to "reckon with aggression"? *Reckoning* suggests deliberate engagement with a savvy challenger. *Reckoning with aggression* means maturing our relationship to aggression, seeking especially to reframe aggression in terms of its ambiguity and relationality and to integrate aggression with love. To be effective, this work on our relationship with our aggression must happen both personally and collectively, and it depends on recurring cycles of growth in three interrelated dimensions of human life: cognition, affect, and practice. One, we must work toward *thinking differently* about aggression, by utilizing a theory of aggression that enables us to conceptualize our aggression more complexly, mutually, honestly, and creatively. Thus, this book critiques and builds on aggression theory and scholarship with the goal of bringing increased scope, balance, and integration to thinking about aggression. Two, we must work toward *feeling differently* about aggression, by making safer spaces together in which to explore our aggression spiritually and psychologically and come to know better—and be more in charge of—our aggressiveness. Thus, this book attempts to provide guidance for building a relationship to aggression that is more soulful, centered, respectful, and wise. Three, we must work toward *behaving differently* in relation to aggression by cultivating practice in aggressiveness that is a "middle way" between too much and not enough aggressiveness, between giving aggression away to others and hoarding it for oneself, and between passivity and violence. Thus, this book tries to show some pathways toward greater mutuality, safety, and support in the inevitable expression of aggression.

An analogy may make this process clearer. Overall, reckoning with aggression is similar to recent efforts to repair our understanding of and relationship to sexuality. Like aggression, human sexuality issues in a broad range of feelings, behaviors, values, and meanings. In recent years some scholars have argued that our understanding of the complex workings of sexuality has become distorted, especially by our inability to keep in focus the complexity and mutuality that characterize healthy sexuality.[9] Analyzing the dangers and losses of this distortion, these scholars have noted that many people have lost touch with the broad spectrum of erotic life, split sex from intimacy, and, in so doing, laid the groundwork for violence. A significant aspect of the distortion is denial of sexuality's ubiquity and multivalent power, and this denial is inextricably linked to problems in sexuality. When mutual, sexuality can be a source of pleasure, but, when misused, sexuality can also be a tool in domination. These scholars are developing strategies intended to increase our consciousness of sexuality, broaden again our understanding of it, and help us return to ethical enjoyment of sexuality's power.

The similarity to my project with aggression is significant. Our experience of these two sources of energy—sexuality and aggression—both complex and mysterious in their essence, has been cut short, mangled, reduced to a caricature of their actual functions. We split off the most positive aspects of these powerful forces from the most dangerous and are left with weapons and wounds. As with sexuality, denial of aggression's existence not only completely fails to eradicate its existence but also inevitably fans its sparks into flames of violence and other problems. We must identify and root out the violence caused through the misuse of these powerful sources of energy. But we must at the same time seek to use these powerful energies—sexuality and aggression—as a source of life. Without them, we perish, literally and spiritually.

This book explores aggression as one partial but, I hope, persuasive answer to problems of violence and vitality. If violence were not a plague among us, and if the need for—and promise of—vitality sufficient to resist violence and live transformatively were not so urgent, then the study of aggression might never have come to my attention.

As I have talked in public forums about the ideas in this book, nearly always someone says that assertion should be our objective, not aggression. I agree that assertion is often an adequate and effective enough expression of aggressiveness. I argue here, however, that effective assertiveness *is* an expression of aggression and that dealing forthrightly with aggression will increase our capacity to be appropriately assertive. We will be more in charge of our reserves of energy, less likely either to underreact or to overreact. In contrast, efforts to bypass dealing with aggression frequently lead to "assertion" that is actually feeble or overbearing. Furthermore, I argue here that, especially from a pastoral theological perspective, assertion is not always a strong enough response to transform suffering and wrongdoing. Assertion might be enough if evil were not so prevalent among us. Stronger expressions of aggression are often-needed tools in the rigorous work of dismantling injustice and providing healing from its trauma.

Overly optimistic attempts to redeem aggression are just as dangerous as violent aggressiveness. Because there is so much violence in the world, it is risky to suggest that there might be some gain in exploring aggression's values. I have a feeling about this book similar to Bonnie Miller-McLemore's sense of her book on work and family: it "defies rules that a good person just does not go around defying lightly."[10] And so, I write carefully. My words could be taken out of context or in other ways misused to incite or rationalize violent aggressiveness. Aggression seems so easily out of control, so quickly hurtful, and so fearsomely primal—Is it not safer to teach resistance of it?

At first glance, it does appear more prudent to keep aggression under wraps. But this has been our strategy, and yet violence continues to grow, and our capacity to live with vitality is needed more and more. Denial of aggression only fuels problems in it, decreasing our ability to resist violence and increasing violence itself. Care-filled attention to how aggression can be contained and expressed constructively is an essential segment of the pathway toward decreased violence. This book is my cautious response to this disconcerting paradox.

1

Problems in Aggression

The way of acquiescence leads to moral and spiritual suicide. The way of violence leads to bitterness in the survivors and brutality in the destroyers.
—Martin Luther King, Jr.,
"My Trip to the Land of Gandhi"

The significance of misplaced aggression is as valid today as it was when I wrote this book. A return of the power of aggression from the destruction of cities and people to assimilation and growth . . . a consummation devoutly to be wished. . . . Bloody unlikely.
—Fritz S. Perls,
Ego, Hunger, and Aggression

In the long run, few people are so bound to ruin friendships and intimate contacts, few arrest their own lives as seriously, and few create in others as deep a sense of entrapment as do passive individuals.
—Edrita Fried, *Active/Passive*

IN *FAREWELL TO ARMS,* Ernest Hemingway observes that "the world breaks everyone and afterward some are strong at the broken places." The truth of his observation is vividly manifest in the strength of many survivors of sociopolitical turmoil and interpersonal abuse. It is just as true, however, that the world breaks everyone, and afterward, many are broken at the strong places. The brokenness in aggression takes many more ambiguous forms, but it is most easily identified in our failure (and the failure of much aggression theory) to find a powerful middle ground between what Martin Luther King, Jr., names "the way of acquiescence" and the "way of violence." It may seem that the destruction identified by

Fritz Perls is the most serious problem in aggression. But our concern and creative interventions need to be directed as much to the quicksand of passivity, where personally and collectively we are smoothly sucked into the ruined relationships, arrested lives, and desperate terror of entrapment observed by Edrita Fried. The mitigation of these problems in aggression is, as Perls fears, "bloody unlikely," only to the degree that we refuse to reckon with aggression. The different thinking, feeling, and behavior described in the introduction can go a very long way toward "the return of the power of misplaced aggression . . . to assimilation and growth."

This chapter explores the brokenness and underdeveloped promise in one source of human strength, aggression. It does so from two perspectives: (1) problems in the living out of aggression and (2) problems in aggression theory that tend not to help—and even exacerbate—the problems in living. The thesis of this chapter is that, to a significant degree, distortions in aggression stem from a collective and personal refusal, in practice and in theory, to contend with the profound ambiguity and relationality that characterize aggression.

A first step in the process of redirecting aggression from negative to positive expressions must be what psychoanalyst Heinz Kohut calls "experience-near" reflection, self-critical contemplation of the feelings and behaviors evoked when we actually encounter aggression's ambiguity and relationality in everyday life.[1] Therefore, in the first part of the chapter, through empathic description, I attempt to create an encounter with and consideration of the affective dimension of these problems—a recollection of what distorted aggression can feel like in a given moment to the people involved. I encourage you to mentally embroider my reflections with your encounters with aggression—yours and others', positive and negative.

A second step in the redirection of aggression is examination of theoretical perspectives on aggression—what Kohut calls "experience-distant" reflection.[2] In the second part of the chapter, I analyze the state of theory development in aggression studies to show that it, too, evidences resistance to the ambiguity and relationality of aggression and thus contributes to problems in aggression. Nonetheless, we find there tools to build a more constructive relationship to our aggression.

Problems in Aggressive Living

The brokenness in our aggression is perhaps most easily identified in its two extremes: violence and passivity, or lack of vitality. At one extreme, aggression explodes into incalculable incidents of hatred and violence. When violent, we are not adequately in charge of our aggression and overuse it, which results in injury and sometimes death. Murderousness—homicide, suicide, hate crimes, random shootings—runs rampant among us. In the death penalty, we see how ineradicable the paradoxical nature of aggression is: "we kill people who kill people to show that killing people is wrong."[3] However, violent aggressiveness has subtle as well as dramatic forms. "You have not seen much of life if you have not seen the hand that kills tenderly," as Friedrich Nietzsche put it.[4] We may avoid committing physical assault, only to take actions that could and sometimes do kill one another's spirits. We may engage in "reckless speech," be habitually faultfinding, always ready for a fight, cruelly withholding, and destructively self-indulgent. Violent assault can come from nearby—on the streets or in families—or from a distance—from governments or boardrooms. The damage it inflicts may be material or spiritual, intentional or collateral.

None of us avoids committing less mortal violences, as our language captures bluntly: we call ourselves character *assassins, cutthroat* competitors, even *kill*joys. Passive-aggressive is a misnomer: the violence in emotional manipulation, sarcasm, and badgering may be indirect, but there is little that is truly passive about it. Some of us are violence voyeurs, and we help build a culture of violence through our appetite for being violence watchers. When we manage to restrain or deny our capacity to be violent against ourselves or others, we are often stalked by the impulse in sleeping and waking fantasies.

Violence is not limited to isolated individuals but infects whole families, brings down entire neighborhoods and congregations, and enforces and perpetuates relationships of domination and subordination between ethnic groups, economic classes, and women and men. Females are violent, and yet violence is especially epidemic among males, who are pressured by socialization to be carriers of combativeness both on behalf of and against females. Violence is perhaps the most terrifying of the viruses for which we have no cure. Thinking theologically about the lack of cure for violence, Marjorie Suchocki contends that the violent tendencies in our aggressiveness, and only secondarily our rebellion against God, create the condition of original sin.[5]

At the other extreme, aggression implodes, a major source of our passion and power drains away, and we are left with too little vitality and vulnerable to too much passivity. When passive, we are not adequately in charge of our aggression and underuse it, resulting in ineffectualness. Extreme lack of aggression has its dramatic and subtle forms, as well. Most dramatically, whole communities are laid low by feelings of helplessness, hopelessness, and apathy. Individuals are clinically catatonic or morbidly depressed. More subtle is the virus of faintheartedness that afflicts the aptly named "silent" majority of us. Legions of us are left feeling worn out and fragile from the demands of life in technological society and present ourselves to our worlds as touchy or timid. Litigious societies have caused a new twist on timidity: while fear of litigation sometimes causes more aggressive behavior, as in healthcare, the threat of suit also leads to excessive caution or even failure to act.[6]

Sometimes our vitality is drained away by violence against us; abuse leaves its victims, in Nancy Ramsay's apt description, "emotionally anemic."[7] In the context of abuse, our attempts to mobilize our power constructively may be squashed by external threats and internal fear or shame.[8] We may struggle but often fail to avoid falling numb and unconscious. We resign ourselves to living captive to fear while our capabilities lie dormant or weakly focused, or we live our lives vicariously, pouring ourselves into the plans of others but not daring to dream a dream for ourselves.

Like violence, passivity and lack of vitality are not limited to isolated individuals but can afflict whole families, lay low entire neighborhoods and congregations, and cause a deadening diffuseness in relationships between ethnic groups, economic classes, and women and men. Our mass dependence on communications media for entertainment and values is not only "cultural conditioning to passivity"[9] but also spiritual submission that has made us audience, not actors. Males sometimes lack vitality, and yet females are especially susceptible to passivity, pressured as they are by socialization to be carriers of pacifism on behalf of males. In all these ways, exhausted or terrified by the demands of freedom, human beings may retreat to dormancy and hibernation. Theologian Susan Nelson has developed a concept that clarifies this brokenness in our aggression theologically. We fall prey to "the sin of hiding," as she calls it, when we seek escape from our freedom in nothingness, in "dissipation," rather than "becoming someone."[10]

The Problem of Splitting

Brokenness in aggression is often, though not always, a sign of the psychological dynamic of splitting. At one level, splitting is our normal and useful capacity to function at more than one plane of consciousness at a time, as in the capacity to think about what to make for dinner while "mindlessly" driving a car. More technically, the psyche has the capacity and tendency to split internalized objects, the ego, and awareness itself (into conscious and unconscious).[11] This tends to happen in the face of ambivalent feelings or external stress or trauma.[12] Most fundamentally, splitting is utilized by the psyche when it is threatened by too much complexity, especially the complexity of ambiguity and relationality. Complexity besets the psyche with confusion and ambivalence, and splitting breaks down reality into parts that are cognitively and emotionally more manageable. Splitting is especially the tendency to respond to the complexities of ambiguity and relationality with either/or thinking, feeling, and behavior: we view people, ideas, and events as either all good or all bad; we focus on the needs of either the self or the other. Splitting and denial enable the personal and collective psyche to think and act on the basis of one-sided, unintegrated, fragmented views.

These and other dualisms can be detected in aggressivity. The extremes of violence and lack of vitality show an all-or-nothing split: on one side is a flood of negativity; on the other side is a bunch of dry bones. Perhaps the most acknowledged split in aggression is between good and bad: aggression is believed to be either evil or imperative, no debate allowed. More dangerous is the split between conscious and unconscious aggression: a person's or group's actual level of aggressiveness can be split off from consciousness. For example, a congregation that prides itself on being friendly can be unconsciously and collectively in denial of its hostility, or the pastor who frets about being too controlling can be experienced by others as weak. Aggression in the self or group is normally split off from aggression in the other: allowed in the self or group and denied in the other, or vice versa. The split between public and private is often visible in aggressive behavior: while an individual or group tends to publicly exhibit one or the other side of the split, privately there is usually a debilitating, dichotomized dialectic, for example, gross entitlement alternating with withering self-hatred. A person who is violent in the home not infrequently has an innocuous public persona, and a person who is entertainingly or obnoxiously aggressive in public may well slump silently in a chair at home.

These splits are etched into social dynamics as well, but even more complexly. Aggression is split along lines of social stratification and mirrors the complexities of relationships of dominance and subordination like racism, sexism, heterosexism, and classism. Dominants have a wide range of aggressive expression in which they can engage with little to no risk, often while maintaining nonaggressive or benignly aggressive personas, while subordinated people are stereotyped as violently or passively aggressive and their healthy aggressivity is ignored, ridiculed, suppressed, or punished. For example, negative stereotypes of passive gay men and aggressive lesbians abound, while the positive aggressiveness both groups have rallied to fight the AIDS epidemic is widely ignored, and the violent aggression of homophobia and heterosexism is masked as "defense of family values."

Our aggression has ruptured along an additional fault line. In the extremities of violence and lack of vitality, we have split off our aggression from love. The notion of a kindly aggressiveness is barely imaginable; the capacity for disciplining without rancor is rare. We wrench the gentleness and respectfulness out of aggression; persistence and resilience are missing from love. In love, we are unable to differentiate; in aggression, we are unable to covenant. We feel too vulnerable when loving and too inflexible when aggressive. For example, a loving couple prides itself on never having an argument, and then, suddenly, one of them wants to end the relationship.

While the splits in aggression and between aggression and love are rarely as complete as I have described, few of us are unfamiliar with these gaps. By these splits, we usually are seeking, perhaps beyond our awareness, to reduce the complexities of aggression's essential ambiguity and relationality. This is an understandable but unreachable goal. The splits do not resolve the problems in aggression. Our groveling niceness becomes as revolting to us as our mean judgmentalism. In the process, we rob our aggression of the very qualities that have the potential to keep it safer and more life-supporting.

What causes this splitting in aggression? Aggression's distortions have numerous causes. However, since we tend to do this "splitting" in reaction to the complexity of ambiguity and relationality, we can hypothesize that one of the foundational causes of problems in aggression is denial of and active resistance against its ambiguity and relationality. What are the threats posed by aggression's ambiguity and relationality? We can barely tolerate aggression's ambiguity—the rush of pleasure we experience when we aggressively defeat another, the shame we feel when we nonaggressively allow another to take advantage of us. We can barely tolerate aggression's relationality—"it takes two," my parents were right to say to me and my siblings, as we each pointed fingers at the other. If we were to take aggression's ambiguity and relationality seriously, the emotional and relational terrain of our lives would shift dramatically and make enormous demands on us.

The Challenges of
Ambiguity and Relationality

As is clear by now, a primary claim underlying this book is that the world in which we live is, in its essence, complexly ambiguous and relational and that well-being rests upon acknowledging, grappling with, and acting in the face of this fundamental reality. By ambiguity, I refer to the condition of multiple meanings and values that characterizes human life. Ambiguity refers to the paradoxical, "both/and" quality of life. It causes the difficulty we face when we must—or feel we must—choose either this or that thing, person, value, or action. Ambiguity increases the more that we make space for difference. Thus, as we become more aware of the universe's plurality, our awareness of ambiguity grows. Ambiguity is intriguing and yet disconcerting. When we cannot observe it from a distance—intrigued with the androgyny of many fashion models and musical artists, for example—we typically push it away.

Yet multiple meanings, apparent contradictions, and mystery contribute to human life much of its depth and value. From a theological point of view, ambiguity's richness of possibility and meaning leads us toward that which is holy. "We know God in and through the ambiguities of our personal and cultural histories," as Marjorie Suchocki puts it.[13] Indeed, ambiguity is not only a way of knowing the sacred but also a quality of sacredness itself, as we experience, for example, in the awe-fulness of birthing and dying. This diversity of sacredness is both blessing and bane.[14] It is, on the one hand, assurance of redemptive possibility in all moments of life. On the other hand, it frustrates the search for any one truth, any one way. In this view, persons and situations are, as one client described it to me, "not much black and white, but a lot of dark white and light black."[15]

Psychologically and socially, the capacity to be conscious of, tolerate, and act in the face of ambiguity and ambivalence is a sign of maturity, an emotional achievement.[16] In ambiguity exists the fluidity and multiplicity of selfhood.

Though some of us seek well-being through development of one unified sense of self, a harmonization of our various aspects, others have discovered the valuable flexibility afforded by choosing to develop several "selves." If they are conscious and authentic constellations of a person's attributes, these different selves provide emotional suppleness for responding effectively to the diverse demands of different social and interpersonal relationships, even as they introduce a not-always-unpleasant ambiguity or a bit of mystery to personal identity. All of us have an "evolving self," psychologist Robert Kegan says. At times we strike with ambiguity what he calls "an evolutionary truce," periods of "dynamic balance." But the self is at all times in "evolutionary motion," a process of development in relational interaction, that Kegan proposes is the "prior (or grounding) phenomenon in personality."[17]

Perhaps more than any other factor, ambiguity's relativity of values challenges us. How can we know what is ethical in the midst of ambiguity? Ethics amid ambiguity does not require erecting unchanging principles but rather an ever-ongoing process of reflection on issues, examination of options for response, and an assessment of the effectiveness of one's action that returns one to reflection and begins the cycle again. "Morality resides in the painfulness of an indefinite questioning,"[18] feminist philosopher Simone de Beauvoir assures us.

We must go further, however. Questioning cannot be an end in itself, or ambiguity an excuse for inaction. As Suchocki observes, "to be faith-full is to accept the challenge of ambivalence and ambiguity by coming to judgments and decisions."[19] Perhaps the greatest gift of the deeply spiritual life is a capacity to hold decisions in an open hand, even while living decisively in an ambiguous world. Given contemporary pressure to be single-minded, it may be helpfully counter-cultural to develop the ability to be what sociologist Andrew Weigert calls "affective heretics," able to act on "one emotion while feeling others of equal strength."[20] In this way we have developed consciousness and tolerance of complexity and, though still ambivalent, we are no longer negatively split and immobilized.

Much of life's ambiguity arises from multiple and sometimes conflicting relational ties and responsibilities. Relationality—the essential interconnectedness of all aspects of creation—leads to plurality of connections, needs, accountability, and responsibilities. Psychologists at the Stone Center at Wellesley College define relationship as "an experience of emotional and cognitive *intersubjectivity*: the ongoing, intrinsic inner awareness and responsiveness to the continuous existence of the other or others and the expectation of mutuality in this regard."[21] We experience many types and levels of this intersubjectivity: in religious or spiritual experience, our most intimate personal relationships, our kinship-style communal relationships, and the web of connections that constitute our ecological relatedness not only to people around the globe but also to all elements of the universe.

In many psychological theories and modes of clinical practice, emphasis on separation and individuation is being balanced with attention to the way a sense of self is formed in the context of relationship.[22] Family systems theorist Murray Bowen claims that three-person relationship, not the socially emphasized couple, is the "molecule" of any emotional system and "the smallest stable relationship system."[23] Psychology and other clinical disciplines have not yet developed adequate language for what could be called the "ecology of selfhood," the deep and broad system of relatedness—biological, economic, psychospiritual—of which we are mostly unconscious.[24] For this, many mental health professionals are turning to ancient disciplines of spiritual and religious practice.

Like ambiguity in general, relationality has a part in the revelation of God. Even in solitude, it is through relationship—to nature, to sacred texts, to silence, to people we encounter unexpectedly—that we encounter the holy. Additionally, contemporary theological constructions increasingly emphasize the interconnectedness of each element of creation, and the connectedness between the creation and God. Process theology envisions everything, God included, as being involved in a complex web of continuously unfolding relationships. In theologian Sallie McFague's metaphor of the world as God's body, God's immanence is highlighted, suggesting God is present in close relationship to the creation. Again, ambiguity appears in relation to the sacred: the image of the sacred body joins the material with the ineffable and bridges a series of philosophical splits—spirit and matter, humanity and nature.[25]

A capacity for tolerating ambiguity and relationality does not come naturally. As we have seen, with their complexities, both ambiguity and relationality represent significant spiritual demands and may even be experienced as threatening, paralyzing, flooding, or fragmenting. If we choose to take on the challenge of grappling with them—and advancing maturation eventually leaves us little choice—we are wisest if we prepare carefully, find ourselves a guide—spiritual director, pastoral counselor, or soul friend—and move slowly. Perhaps the greatest challenge is that if we acknowledge the extent of ambiguity and relationality, we must relativize—while not minimizing—ourselves and our own concerns. Literature and activism that call for increased openness to pluralism too frequently underestimate or even ignore the psychospiritual challenges of making ourselves vulnerable to complexity and connection. Increased openness to the ambiguity and relationality of cultural multiplicity depends upon psychospiritual strategies no less than upon social strategies.

Reckoning with aggression is one way to avoid romanticizing either ambiguity or relationality. Taking seriously the challenge and value of ambiguity and relationality would have tremendous implications for dealing with problems in aggression. We would have to give up the notion that nonaggressiveness is the holy way. Instead, we would have to wrestle with the multiplicity of aggression's values until a blessing emerged. We would have to acknowledge that people cannot be categorized into aggressive and nonaggressive, goats easily distinguishable from sheep. Instead, maturity would rest on one's ability to find an appropriate decisiveness and balance in aggressive behavior. The aggression a person expressed would no longer be seen as absolutely defensible or condemnable. Instead, we would embrace the complexity that aggression is not good or bad but always and all at once helpful and harmful. We would have to give up self-righteousness, self-blame, and scapegoating in regard to aggression and, instead, develop much more sophisticated and complex ways of assessing and responding to aggression's values and costs.

We would have to give up the illusion that self and other are largely distinguishable and independent. Instead, we would exercise our aggression and measure its value as much for its effects on "us" as on "me." We would have to give up the search for the one thing or group or quality to blame for aggression—media or mothers, genes or gangs—and reconcile ourselves to the awareness that aggression never happens in a vacuum, in isolation, but always happens between persons, and secondary to a variety of causes. We would have to give up the search for one responsible party—teachers, parents, churches—onto whom to shift responsibility for change in aggressiveness. Instead, we would have to build coalitions, probably with people we do not like or with whom we do not agree. We would have to give up our exclusive focus on curtailing violent aggression. Instead, we would have to work at giving one another opportunities to practice being constructively aggressive.

Possibilities and Problems
in Aggression Theory

If we turn to aggression theory for help with these problems in aggression, we enter into both promising possibilities and a huge, fragmented, and confusing territory that poses additional problems. I work on two primary tasks throughout this section. First, I survey the major strands of aggression theory—their main characteristics, values, and limitations. This overview serves both as an initial step in the multidisciplinary approach to aggression that I am arguing is essential and, for those who are not specialists in aggression theory, as an orientation to the range of contemporary approaches. Due to the quantity of literature on aggression and the limitations of space, my characterizations here are necessarily broad. But at least a sketch and initial assessment of these theories is essential for constructing an informed theological understanding of aggression. In chapter 2, I utilize some of these approaches and theorists in more detail. Also, through my assessments of these theories, I articulate the principles that guide my selective utilization of these approaches in chapter 2, where I construct a broad characterization of aggression.

Depth Psychology

As I mentioned in the introduction, my discovery of depth psychological writings on aggression was the first—and one of the most transformative—steps in the direction of the present study.[26] Depth psychological approaches to aggression have several particular characteristics and values. First and foremost, in these writings, aggression's ambiguity and relationality are emphasized. We use our aggression to do both good and harm, and we utilize it to build both positive and negative connections with others. Second, in most depth psychological literature, the study of aggression leads to—and requires—examination of healthy as well as unhealthy expressions of agency and power. For many of these theorists, to speak about aggression is to try to capture in words human vitality, the nearly indestructible psychobiological will to survive and thrive that animates us and causes us to act in defense of life—our own and others'. Psychoanalyst Clara Thompson's position is typical of this point of view: Aggression "springs from the tendency to grow and master life which seems to be characteristic of all living matter."[27]

Third, depth psychology assists us in understanding why we use our aggression violently and how that violence arises in the midst of relationship. From this point of view, aggression can turn violent in the face of real or perceived threat to one's own survival or thriving, or that of one's "loved ones"—treasured people, things, places, ideas, and principles. Thompson continues: "Only when this life force [aggression] is obstructed in its development do ingredients of anger, rage, or hate become connected to it."[28] In its study of aggression turned to violence, depth psychology attends not only to physical violence but also goes much further, detailing and decrying the aggressive violence in rage, emotional cruelty, relational withdrawal, and even neglect.

Depth psychology's attention to aggression is also distinctive among aggression theories because its emphasis is clinical and affective. It comes to the study of aggression from the perspective of attempting to help people pained by the complexities of psychospiritual life, a crucial aspect for a pastoral theological approach to aggression. These clinician-theorists attend extensively to the costs suffered when all aggressiveness is repressed. "If society is in danger," D. W. Winnicott says, "it is not because of man's aggressiveness but because of the repression of personal aggressiveness in individuals."[29] Since neither banishment nor repression is a viable remedy, it is incumbent upon us to develop maturity in the expression of aggression. Maturity in aggressiveness includes the ability to control it and to exercise aggression in conscious, life-affirming, and contextually appropriate ways.

Finally, the plausibility and imperative of these depth psychological views of aggression and their importance for spiritual life and theological reflection and praxis are increased by the fact that, more than any other approach, these views do justice to the range of meanings attributed to aggression in popular language and common wisdom. When I began to listen, I realized that those who speak and write in English use *aggression* and *aggressiveness* with thick ambiguity, in reference to situations, actions, qualities, and problems ranging from war to sports, murder to heroics, abrasiveness to directness, and violence to vitality. Additionally, common usage suggests that aggression is not simply mine or yours but arises as much between us, in the context of relationship: we refer to the aggressiveness of a team, of the political climate, and of certain approaches to evangelization. The broad range of meanings attributed to aggression may well reflect the actual complexity of human experience in relation to aggressiveness. Depth psychology's conceptualization of aggression enables us to understand why aggression is conceived of so broadly. Moreover since linguistic connotations arise in the context of social dynamics of domination and subordination, it is crucial to study both formal and popular meanings attributed to aggression,[30] and depth psychology makes such an approach possible.

In addition to these strengths, there are problems in depth psychological approaches to aggression. First, while I have characterized the majority of depth psychologists as typically defining *aggression* as a neutral or ambiguous and relational force, there are those theorists who, following the spirit if not the letter of Sigmund Freud's theory of instinctual violence,[31] focus on aggression's violences.[32] Some continue to imply an innate destructiveness,[33] despite the strong opinion of a majority of researchers that there is no scientific evidence of an instinct for violence.[34] Study of the destructive potential of the aggressive drive is valuable for its unswerving attention to the human capability to do violence, often long after—or seemingly even without—provocation. But we can attend to the destructive uses of aggression without imputing to it—without evidence—an inherent destructiveness. Characterizations that unnecessarily imply innate destructiveness can cultivate a pessimistic, irresponsible attitude toward aggressiveness in that the innate cannot be changed. They thus demonstrate and contribute to the neglect of aggression's ambiguity and relationality.

An additional problem in depth psychological approaches to aggression is the insufficiency of social analysis and thus the circumventing of the broadest aspects of aggression's relationality. Though depth psychology provides tools for social analysis, many who utilize the theory do not pay adequate attention to the social, economic, and political forces resulting from and impacting human aggressiveness. For example, object relations theorists offer extensive and crucial analysis of the significance of aggression in the interpersonal relationship between mother and child. Yet the violent aggressiveness of racism and sexism in the mother's and child's social context and possible effects on their aggressiveness—arguably another unavoidable dimension of object relations— are barely mentioned.[35]

Social Sciences

The examination of aggression in social psychology, cross-cultural psychology, and anthropology yields still more promising insights into aggression. Most researchers in these fields take great pains to distance themselves from Freud's notion of a violently aggressive instinct, but the majority follow him in defining aggression negatively. In these disciplines, *aggression* is typically defined as intent to harm,[36] and thus research yields detailed insights into violence. (Indeed, these studies would be better named *violence studies*.) As we will see, there is significant advantage in defining *aggression* as intent to harm, since it keeps our attention riveted to the damage we do with our aggression. By excluding all other meanings, it firmly directs analysis toward the real costs paid so frequently for the expression of aggression. Here we also find valuable empirical research on the ways violent aggression is learned.[37] This is a more optimistic approach than those that focus on innate destructiveness: if violent behavior can be learned, then it is reasonable to surmise that *nonviolence* can be learned as well.

Social-scientific approaches began with the 1939 publication of the findings of a group of Yale scientists, who moved the study of aggressive behavior into the laboratory and demonstrated that frustration can cause negative aggression.[38] Later research was to make clear that the frustration-aggression hypothesis was not sufficient to explain all destructive aggressiveness, since not all frustration results in aggression, nor is frustration the only cause of aggression. But the behavioral orientation of the Yale group and their attempt to study aggression scientifically set in motion a valuable new emphasis in aggression studies: empirical measurement of the ways that cognitive responses to external reinforcement work together to elicit negative aggression.

Aggression theory underwent another major innovation in 1973, when Albert Bandura proposed what he called a *social learning theory:* negative aggression is learned and maintained like any other new behavior, Bandura found, through imitative behavior modeled after socializing agents (such as parents, peers, teachers, and media and advertising) and through positive rewards.[39] In order to explain why some people are more violently aggressive than others, social cognitive theory later offered a fine-tuning. We all learn patterns of behavior (aggressive and otherwise) social cognitive theorists call *cognitive scripts,* and we are influenced by rewards or punishments for harmful aggressive behavior based on internalized norms learned early in life. Children who learn that violent aggressiveness is acceptable are more likely to use their violent aggressive scripts.[40]

This arena of study provides another important tool in social interactionist theory. It enables study of the "ecology of aggression": the web of person-environment interactions at micro-, meso-, and macrolevels that produces negatively aggressive behavior.[41] Additionally, we find in this strand of aggression theory cross-cultural, ethnological, and anthropological studies.[42] These approaches are valuable for their effort to understand the meaning of aggression within specific cultural contexts by observing and talking with people who live in those cultures.

Problems in the social-scientific study of aggression center first on issues of definition. There are several problems in defining *aggression* as "intent to harm." Rather than taking seriously the range of meanings attributed to aggression in everyday speech and in social representations, most aggression researchers dismissively attribute it to "fuzzy thinking" and error; they arbitrarily choose the more focused, less ambiguous definition on the basis of its suitability for their research purposes.[43] The focus on intent fails to assist us in dealing with aggression's ambiguity or its relationality: most study is of the *harmful* behavior of *individual* actors. This results in a definition of *aggression* that is narrow, somewhat artificial, and thus of limited value in illuminating the everyday experience of aggression.[44] Additionally, little distinction is made in these studies between aggression and violence.[45] To use *aggression* to talk about violence makes *aggression* a camouflage word for violence. Where there is violence, we should name it as such. Some of these researchers admit that, paradoxically, despite their focus on intent to harm and violence, the most scientific laboratory studies of aggression do not capture the most virulently violent reactions, even though these are the most troubling and costly.[46] Finally, the focus on violent aggressiveness leads to virtually exclusive attention to pathology. Negligible attention is given in this strand of aggression theory to how aggression might be handled more constructively and to the healthy human agency required for resisting violent behavior.

Another set of problems relates to the limitations of scientific method and findings. People not trained in science may reverence it, unaware of the significant problems the researchers themselves sometimes admit. More than the nonscientific are aware, empirical research is art as well as science. Many scientific studies rely on self-reporting, and their results can be distorted by the subjects' conscious or unconscious misrepresentation of their aggressiveness.[47] Scientific findings are sometimes contradictory or quickly called into question by subsequent findings. One problem only recently admitted is the exclusivistic bent of many scientific approaches to aggression studies and the rarity of the multidisciplinary approach necessary for the understanding of aggression's complexity.[48] Finally, scientific studies of aggression widely claim to be objective and value-free. But observational method, long a cornerstone of scientific study, is currently being shown to inject researcher bias into laboratory and field studies and thus distort findings. For example, traditional studies of gender and aggression, most of which have been conducted by men, have measured aggression through direct actions that cause injury to another. On this basis, females have for decades been reported to be less aggressive than males. More recently, Finnish scientist Kirsti Lagerspetz and her research team have studied aggression in females but included in their definition aggression that is indirect, expressed, for example, through maligning others behind their backs. In their studies, females appear as aggressive as males.[49]

Biological Sciences

Examination of the physiology of aggression also provides critical insights into aggression. This research, too, is directed nearly exclusively to violent aggressiveness, not to the physiology of constructive aggressiveness. Though they no longer talk about instinct, some biologists seem not to have given up the search for a first or primary cause for violence in the body.

The major value of these approaches is that through neuroscience we can study in much more detail the relationship between violent aggressiveness and the body. For example, some organic pathology in the brain and other areas of the body can cause violent behavior without provocation.[50] In addition, these approaches extensively study the automatic functioning of the ancient limbic system—seat of the fight-flight mechanism—and its power to evoke in us aggressive behavior. In this way, the human brain is "prewired" for violent aggression but generally requires the stimulation of environment before violence is evoked.[51] Physiological aspects of aggression are not all impulse, however. The neocortex—the area of the brain used for thinking and problem solving—is used in acts of violence planned in advance. Finally, physical discomfort has been shown to elicit aggressiveness and infliction of injury.[52]

Research in the physiology of violent aggression has offered some evidence of a positive correlation between aggression and the male sex hormone testosterone.[53] However, new findings confound this long-held belief. Recent evidence shows that a *deficiency* of testosterone, not only an excess, can contribute to negative aggressiveness. Additionally, there are indications that the female sex hormone estrogen also contributes to negative aggressiveness.[54] While there seems to be some relationship between sex hormones and negative aggressiveness, researchers are far from proving that relationship. At most, we can posit that sex hormones organize the brain to respond to stimuli in a particular way, but not that sex hormones activate or cause negative aggressiveness. Sex differences in aggression are not actualized except in response to environmental stimuli.

Other areas of research show that environmental toxins—lead in house paint, for example—may contribute more to violent aggression than recent social science approaches have allowed.[55] Finally, though the findings are limited and also disputed, there is some research evidence, obtained through the study of twins reared apart from each other, that violent aggression may have a genetic basis.[56] The best assessment at this point indicates that genetic influence constitutes a potential for the development of a very specific type of aggressive behavior—criminal tendencies—which is only sometimes triggered in response to environment and learning.

There are several problematic issues in physiological studies of aggression. Again, focus on aggression's violence seems to derail attention from the physiological processes that underlie, or could help to strengthen, a person's sense of vitality. Thus, they fail to provide tools for fostering more ambiguity in our embodiment of aggression. Further, there is no way to completely rule out the effects of socialization, even in twin and other genetic studies, and therefore no way to be sure that findings regarding the biology of aggression are not in actuality evidence of the effect of environment. Indeed, some of these methods seek to study the body extrapolated from its environment and thus study an artificial body, not the profound mutual interaction of biology, relationship, and culture that together give form to actual human embodiment. Moreover, social analysis is rare in these approaches. While physiological research can tell us a great deal about aggressive response, it can tell us very little about the relationship between response and the object or person that is the target of that response, and thus the "aggression" it reveals is an individualized aggression. Further, research in physiology may play into the temptation to reductionism—the desire to find an "aggression bullet," one cause for or solution to the tormenting problem of violence. Alternatively, since this line of inquiry suggests a significant physiological basis for violent aggression, it can be interpreted to imply that our capacity or responsibility for controlling aggression is limited. This can lead, in turn, to a pessimistic, demoralizing, and erroneous sense that violent aggression cannot be significantly affected by intervention.

Theology

Unspoken injunctions against aggression exist in the culture of many Christian churches.[57] They are also directly stated in theological reflection. On the rare occasions that aggression is explicitly discussed in theology, it is often characterized as destructive and therefore sinful. Two examples suffice. No one has written more about aggression in the theological literature than pastoral psychologist David W. Augsburger. He helpfully reviews the range of aggression theories[58] and then, without explanation, aligns himself with social learning theories that define *aggression* as intent to harm.[59] Theologically, he characterizes aggression as "loveless power."[60] He offers helpful discussions of the relationality and ambiguity in phenomena like assertiveness, anger, conflict, and confrontation,[61] but their relationship to aggression is not sufficiently clarified.[62] Theologian Marjorie Suchocki develops an extensive argument that aggressive tendencies are built into human nature.[63] However, no doubt because the focus of her book is on the doctrine of original sin, she does not explore the positive potential of those innate aggressive tendencies but devotes her attention to their close relationship to violence.

It is interesting to note, however, that especially in the period of the late 1950s through the early 1970s, some religious and theological writers embraced a broader conceptualization of aggression and raised the possibility that aggression might have some value for theological reflection and the life of faith. In the development of nonviolence theory, Gandhi spoke to the necessity of "aggressive civil disobedience,"[64] and Martin Luther King, Jr., argued that the effectiveness of nonviolence rests in large measure on proponents who are "dynamically aggressive spiritually."[65] A small flurry of articles appeared in the 1960s and early 1970s,[66] for which the civil rights movement, the Vietnam War, the antiwar movement, and the publication of Konrad Lorenz's widely noted study, *On Aggression,*[67] were likely precipitants. The authors voiced similar concerns: the lack of attention given to aggression in theology, the inability of many persons of faith to mobilize aggression constructively or morally, and, most foundationally, the role of healthy aggressiveness in religious integrity. As Jesuit priest, psychiatrist, and psychoanalyst William W. Meissner put it, "the virtues of zeal, fortitude, [and] perseverance are meaningless without consideration of the aggressive component that gives them vitality."[68] Since then, only Ann and Barry Ulanov's challenging exposition of aggression and prayer has substantively extended discussion in the theological literature of aggression's ambiguity and relationality.[69]

Emerging concurrently with this group of writings, liberation theologies only occasionally use the language of aggression explicitly. But the language used in theologies of liberation—feminist, African American, womanist, and *mujerista,* for example—is suggestive of constructive aggressiveness and implies that constructive aggressiveness, used to strengthen the web of relationship, is a crucial aspect of the liberation dynamic. Three themes commonly encountered in liberation theologies—agency, anger, and perseverance—exemplify this literature's allusions to aggression. First, significant human agency or passion is required for the repair of the world. "Apart from miracles," theologian Virginia Ramey Mollenkott argues, "how would God's will be done on earth if not through human agency?" Human responsibility requires "*godding,*" Mollenkott asserts, "an embodiment or incarnation of God's love in human flesh, with the goal of cocreating with God a just and loving human society."[70] Second, anger is understood to have ethical value. Ethicist Beverly Wildung Harrison's often-quoted article, "The Power of Anger in the Work of Love," reframes anger as "a mode of connectedness to others" that signals "resistance" to immoral social relations and can be a "vivid form of caring."[71] Finally, perseverance is a central requirement for the resistance of evil. New Testament scholar Elsa Tamez calls attention to the "militant, heroic patience" acclaimed in the Epistle of James, which means "to persevere, to resist, to be constant, unbreakable, immovable."[72]

A very distinctive problem characterizes theological approaches in aggression studies and limits the helpfulness of many theological understandings in our project of reckoning with aggression's ambiguity and relationality: theological literature is profoundly inconsistent with regard to aggression.[73] For example, most major religions call people of faith to control their violent aggressiveness. But scriptures and the histories of many religious communities and individuals record countless episodes of murderousness and emotional cruelty, often justified through appeal to divine example and sanction. Further, though violent aggressiveness is decried, it has long been a barely concealed staple in the tools of evangelism. My search of the Claremont library database for any theological book that had the word "aggression" or "aggressive" in its title yielded only one, a slim volume called *Papers on Aggressive Christianity*. It is the publication of a series of addresses given in the West End of London in the summer of 1880 by the Salvation Army's Mrs. General Catherine Booth. Trying to rouse her listeners to evangelistic zeal in converting nonbelievers, she exhorted them to

> not rest content with just putting it [the gospel] before them, giving them gentle invitations, and then leaving them alone . . . knock and hammer and burn in, with the fire of the Holy Ghost, your words into their poor darkened hearts, . . . Go after them. . . .[74]

Like Booth's words, contemporary evangelistic aggressiveness is too often violent in its rhetoric, moral judgmentalism, and spiritual invasiveness and presumptuousness. Attempts to persuade that belittle, attack, or otherwise damage the spiritual well-being of another meet our criteria for violence, and this is true whether the persuasion has a "conservative" or "liberal" rationale.

Religious traditions also normally call their adherents to live joyfully, boldly, and, because of violence, resistively. I suggest that this call to tremendously powerful, effective living can be understood, in part, as a call to "healthy" or "constructive" aggressiveness. Here, too, however, there is inconsistency. In Christianity, for example, the story of Jesus tossing tables around the temple (Mark 11:15–18) is beloved, but admonitions to follow the example of Jesus are widely assumed to exclude such aggressive behavior. Preaching and teaching urge listeners into forceful prophetic witness, but Christian communities are often quick to judge and marginalize as "too aggressive" those who name injustice forcefully, make unconventional choices, or assert themselves boldly. Biblical images like those of the persistent widow (Luke 18:1–8) invite women and men to be lovingly tenacious in inquiring about important matters of faith. But in many Christian circles, we will not recognize love in any strong debate or witness, even when it is present in the form, for example, of respectfulness and nonviolence. In too many communities any disagreement is felt to be too aggressive, not loving, unchristian. Is it not antithetical to the relationship modeled by Jesus and his followers, however, if our spiritual bonds and well-being are so fragile that we cannot brave and learn from differences and disagreements that refine and thus nurture relationship?

Despite the biblical call to constructive powerfulness, many of our communities of faith are plagued with serious problems in demoralization, diffuseness, even deadness, suggesting a desperate need for vitality and even (constructive forms of) aggressiveness.[75] The somnolence that can overtake us when even healthy aggression is deemed unacceptable makes it nearly impossible to analyze and resist evil. We have not given enough attention to how we are to develop the power to which we are called.

In these theological inconsistencies, we encounter a problem I address shortly: although aggressive behavior is ostensibly questionable for everyone, persons in dominant groups are penalized less for their aggressiveness while aggressiveness for persons in subjugated groups is highly risky. But most marginalized persons have not had the luxury of nonaggressiveness: most have had to use aggressiveness—often in creative and subtle forms—to survive and subvert systems of oppression. The history of slavery in the United States provides a clear example. Whites, many of them Christian and espousing holiness, openly inflicted a system of violent aggression on captured Africans and punished any open aggressiveness by which African slaves attempted to free themselves. This use of aggression to quell aggression—violence to quell rebellion—gave rise to a subtle system of resistance among slaves and their supporters. For example, the underground railroad was clearly an aggressive undertaking, full of risk and savvy subversion of slavery. These inconsistencies in theological interpretations and assessments of aggression need to be identified and studied, so that the dangers, challenges, and necessity of aggression can be encountered openly in communities of faith.

Gender and Ethnic Studies

When we examine how aggression is regarded in discussions where gender and race are central issues, attention to the potential harmful and unjust use of aggression is not lessened, but aggression's meanings and functions are assessed in cultural context, with particular attention to social or interpersonal arrangements of power and privilege. A "politics of aggression" emerges, revealing three levels of significance for aggression: (1) socialization creates variable meanings and functions for aggression according to one's position(s) in domination-subjugation dynamics, (2) domination is enforced with violent aggressiveness, and (3) aggression is used by the subjugated as a tool in resistance to domination.[76] Thus, some gender and ethnic theory sees the recovery of healthy aggressiveness as a necessary tool in resisting and dismantling sexism and racism.[77]

Through these approaches, we are able to see how aggression is gendered.[78] Through socialization, aggression is allowed to or even forced on men, while denied to or mocked in women. As practical theologian James Newton Poling puts it, "to the extent that aggression splits into rage and helplessness, this split corresponds to the social expectations for men and women under patriarchy."[79]

These approaches also reveal how aggression is racialized.[80] Ironically, that

aggression is racialized is clearly revealed whenever white feminists make gen-
eralizations about women's need to reclaim aggression. White women have
sometimes had the luxury of sacrificing their aggressiveness because they could
rely on the largesse and protection of aggressive white men. Feminist analysis
makes clear that seeking to reclaim or practice aggressiveness is an issue for
many white women. But, as black feminist and womanist writers make plain,
contemporary African American women and their foremothers never had the luxury of nonaggressiveness. They have normally had to be aggressive as a matter
of survival because of slavery and racism (though they could mask it, if strategic,
when dealing with whites). Sojourner Truth's beloved words of protest, spoken
in 1852 to the second annual convention of the women's rights movement—over
the protests of white women who shouted their objections to her speaking—il-
lustrate aggressiveness rallied in words and in actions to fight both racism and
sexism.[81]

> Look at me! Look at my arm! . . . I have plowed, and planted, and gath-
> ered into barns, and no man could head me—and ain't I a woman? I
> could work as much as any man (when I could get it), and bear de lash
> as well—and ain't I a woman? I have borne five children and I seen
> 'em mos all sold off into slavery, and when I cried out with a woman's
> grief, none but Jesus hear—and ain't I a woman?[82]

People of color echo Sojourner Truth's sentiments through the generations.
Aggression is understood as a tool in both enforcement of racism and resistance to it. Qualities of aggressiveness are also being reclaimed either explicitly or by allusion for the enlivening of liberation movements around the world,
where it plays a crucial role in the recovery of self-esteem and community
pride, in perseverance *en la lucha*—in the struggle—and, where reform fails,
in revolution.[83] Because aggression has been politicized, the pathologizing of
aggressiveness and unilateral calls for the forfeiture of aggression must be
viewed with suspicion, and the development of constructive aggressive resistance must be encouraged.

One problem that can be identified in theories that analyze aggression's
role in relationships of domination and subordination is that they sometimes
focus so much on self-defensive aggression as a justified response to threat
that, where self-defense turns violent, the long-term cost of that retributive
violence is obscured or minimized.[84] Other problems are more specific to
feminist theories of aggression. First, there are exceptions, but feminist theory tends to promote the popular notion that violence is a male problem,
that men are more aggressive—read *violent*—than women, despite the significant and growing body of research evidence to the contrary. A second
problem is related to the first: there is a rather naive rhetoric in some parts
of the feminist movement about women's essential gentleness and peace-
fulness. There are exceptions, but feminists do not tend to argue against the

popular notion that females are gentle and nurturing by nature, essentially nonaggressive and nonviolent. This leads to a third problem: feminist theories of aggression are marred by only minimal attention to women's violence; some who have tried to open this discussion have been ostracized.[85] Finally, the inconsistent messages and contradictory understandings that plague theological discussions of aggression show up in feminist theory as well. While feminist women tend to be in strong agreement about the violence in aggression, and some call for the shaping of constructive aggressiveness, other feminist theory continues to characterize aggression negatively. For example, self-in-relation theory, arguably one of the most influential feminist psychologies to date, defines *aggression* as "the intent to be destructive to others or to control others through force"[86] and fails to give women's aggression substantive attention.

This brief investigation into the study of aggression in various disciplines reveals that there are crucial perspectives in all of them. At the same time, there are problems in each and no holistic view in any of them. While expert specialization has its place, we also need a coherent picture of aggression that yields guidelines useful in responding to aggression's ambiguity and relationality in daily life. The construction of a broad conceptualization of aggression, by selective utilization of perspectives from these approaches, is our task in the next chapter.

2

What Is Aggression?

Aggression has been a fundamental problem of human experience in all cultures and at all points in human history. How one understands the origins of aggression determines one's positions on many of the most problematic features of life: historical, philosophical, political, and theological.
—Stephen A. Mitchell,
Hope and Dread in Psychoanalysis

HOW ONE UNDERSTANDS AGGRESSION influences not only one's positions but also one's actions—or failure to act—in response to some of the most problematic features of life. In this chapter I use social-scientific theory to begin to construct an understanding of major emotional and relational dynamics in aggressiveness. My goal is to distill the essence of these aggression theories into a conceptualization complex enough to do justice to the diverse meanings attributed to aggression and simple enough to be usable for theological reflection and ethical action in response to aggression.

In this chapter, I utilize a variety of perspectives, but none more than those of object relations theorist Donald Woods Winnicott. Winnicott's theory of aggression, in my view, is the most profound in the psychological literature because it makes the most sense of aggression's multiple meanings and contexts as they are expressed and experienced in everyday life. Further, Winnicott's method is uniquely useful because, in contrast to some of the approaches we have considered, it is not exclusivistic. Winnicott attends to health and suffering, intrapsychic and relational experience, environment and inheritance. Because of this, his theory offers a framework that accommodates a multidisciplinary approach to aggression. This is crucial because, for all its strengths, Winnicott's theory is not adequate in itself. Reckoning with aggression's ambiguity and relationality requires that we give up a "monoexplanatory" approach[1]—the search in aggressiveness for any one source, meaning, or actor. Aggression and its manifestations are multidetermined, and interventions must be multidimensional. I am not seeking to construct one theory of aggression but to knit the best of our knowledge about aggression into as coherent a whole as possible, while avoiding reductionism.

As I have noted, and explore in greater depth in chapter 4, aggression's messages and effects can be fully discerned only by examining the specific cultural and relational contexts in which it arises. This chapter seeks a partial articulation: What might be the basic dynamics in aggression that are to a degree similar in most human beings? Winnicott offers a simple construct to guide us through the maze of aggression's many meanings to a potentially common core. "Put in a nutshell," he says, aggression has two meanings: it is one of two main sources of an individual's energy, and it is a response to frustration or threat.[2] I will explore these meanings in three sections. In the first section, I consider aggression's roots in the body at birth. In the second section, I examine how the groundwork for the development of healthy adult aggressiveness can be laid in childhood. Even in the face of everyday disappointments and more wounding personal and social traumas, in some people aggression develops to be primarily constructive and healthy. I focus here on qualities of relationship that must be provided to children's aggressiveness if adults are truly committed to building nonviolently vital societies. In the third section, I investigate how intense, ongoing abuse contributes to the emergence of violent aggressiveness. I argue a claim on which the majority of my discussion of aggression rests: one major cause of violence is suppression of constructive aggressiveness.

The Roots of Aggression in the Body: Vitality

Two drives—one erotic, the other aggressive—provide energy for living, Winnicott suggests.[3] The aggressive drive does not inherently cause harm but is an ambiguous source of energy for living.[4] To articulate the most foundational nature of the aggressive drive, "it would be necessary to go back to the impulses of the foetus, to that which makes for movement rather than for stillness, to the aliveness of tissues. . . . We need a term here such as life force."[5]

Three notions are central in Winnicott's understanding of the aggressive drive: the primacy of, and relationship between, erotic and aggressive energies; the "life force," or vitality; and movement. Later I address the violence that we can do with aggression, but here we will explore the healthy essence of these aspects of aggression.

The Kinship
of Aggression and Love

At birth, all living things are endowed with what we shall call a psycho-biological impulse to survive and thrive (the impulse to self- and species-preservation).[6] Erotic and aggressive energies are essentially interrelated expressions of this impulse to survive and thrive. We can see this in infants, who have at birth both the sentiment to engage others and the force, especially through their ability to cry, to implore the powerful others around them to do what will enable infants to survive and thrive. How are aggressive and erotic energies interrelated? Winnicott frequently describes aggression and love as "fused."[7] This interrelatedness exists at birth and continues throughout our lives, though often without our conscious awareness or use of it.[8] Aggression and love are fused, not in the sense of being rigidly welded to one another, but in the sense of being indelibly associated, like blood relations.

Kinship is a fitting image to use for the interrelatedness of aggressive and erotic energies. Like our relationships with blood kin, the relationship between love and aggression must be nurtured if it is to mature and be resilient.

Also like our relationships with blood kin, the relationship between love and aggression is often strained, not infrequently distant, even sometimes displeasing or completely estranging. Under optimal conditions—most simply, whenever threats to the self and its affiliations are not too great—we can experience and build up the close relationship between love and aggression. As I discuss below, when the self or its affiliations are threatened, the relationship between love and aggression may break down. Love and aggression may both become either passive or violent. But, in my view, as with blood kin, the essential relatedness of love and aggression, and at least our body-memory of their initial closeness, can never be fully dissolved.

When functioning in this essential unity, aggression and love cannot be fully differentiated. However, an approximation of their particular contributions might be that love is "desire" and, as discussed later, aggression is "movement." Love and aggression function in this braided way because, under favorable conditions, a mixture of love and aggression most effectively ensures personal and collective survival and fullness of life. When integrated, one cooperatively enlivens, seasons, and tempers the other: aggression enables love to move toward the thing desired; love enables aggression to desire the thing toward which it moves. Our love has gumption in it; our aggression has affection in it. Without this intermingling, our love might be passive and our aggression only self-serving; with this intermingling, aggression is more likely to be constructive and love more likely to have fortitude.

The close relationship between erotic and aggressive energies makes plain that the impulse to survive and thrive arises not only on behalf of ourselves but also on behalf of others, especially those we love. We want to survive and thrive with others. Winnicott focuses on the individual and interpersonal, but his conceptualization of aggression enables us to identify qualities of aggressiveness within groups and communities as well as within individuals. Collectives of all sizes—families, neighborhoods, congregations, countries—have an essential desire to survive and thrive as a group, and that impulse is expressed through aggression on the part of individuals within the collective and through joint action.

Aggression as
Life Force and Vitality

Winnicott describes the life force as part of the impulse to survive and thrive.[9] Thus, aggression, or life force, is part of the impulse to survive and thrive, though this essential meaning is frequently deeply unconscious and not easily recognized because of aggression's costs and stigma.[10] As an expression of the life force, our aggression is a source of vitality. This is the foundational level of aggression suggested by my working definition in the introduction. When relatively unobstructed, human aggression manifests in minimally disruptive forms like vigor, agency, enterprise, boldness, and resilience. We are using our aggression (and, for aggression to be constructive, our love as well) when we allow ourselves to be animated, assertive, impassioned, and daring. Our aggressive vitality flowers in struggle and achievement, in "competence strivings."[11] Because of its roots in the impulse to survive, aggression's vitality enables us to endure and empowers us to be persistent. Our aggressive impulse is nearly indefatigable, an implacable desire to be, and be vibrant, and be strong. Aggression is not all we want, but it is part of what we want.

To say that aggression is a drive is not to imply that we do not experience aggression as an affect or emotion.[12] Daniel Stern's notion of "vitality affects"[13] helps make this clear. "Feelings of vitality" arise in relation to "vital processes of life." Stern is thinking of infants, and so he names breathing, hunger, eating, elimination, and sleeping as examples, but we can add vital processes of adult life—sex, work, and play. Vitality affects share the felt quality of a "rush" rather than particular content.[14]

> These elusive qualities are . . . captured by dynamic, kinetic terms, such as "surging," "fading away," "fleeting," "explosive," "crescendo," "decrescendo," "bursting," "drawn out."[15]

Aggression as Movement

As these qualities show, movement is one of the most important aspects of aggression's vitality. Because the aggressive impulse is psychobiological, physical and psychospiritual forms of aggressiveness are indelibly entwined. In the beginning of life, Winnicott says, aggressiveness is "almost synonymous with activity," with the body's capacity for and tendency toward movement.[16] Aggression makes us restless, want to stretch and walk and get "muscle pleasure."[17] Aggression underlies our "basic need for activeness."[18] Movement is a sign of life and of vitality, and it is one the most valuable commodities imparted to us by our aggression. Karen Horney puts at the center of her theory of self the notion that a balance of three *movements*—away from, against, and toward other people—enables the real self to emerge and grow.[19] Without aggression, we move neither toward, away from, or against relationship or an authentic self. Importantly, the movement imparted by aggression leads to well-being not only for individuals but also for relationship. Self-in-relation theorists Jean Baker Miller and Janet Surrey claim that movement is the "essential feature" of relationships that are not static but growing and thus basically healthy.[20]

This notion of aggression fosters a closer, more holistic relationship to the body. The body is not caricatured as the source of an inherently dangerous aggression but is identified as a fount of vital energy—its strength necessary for life, its pleasure often compelling—and it begs for employment and expression. Winnicott's attention to the relation between body and mind also reminds us to take responsibility for a potential danger in aggression: the powerful force of aggression in each of us is not just a psychological force but a physical force. The connectedness of body and emotion means that the roiling psychological aspects of our aggression can transmute, with relative ease and swiftness, into physical expression. Aggressiveness—the movement of a person's life force—is forceful and can be hurtful, however unintentionally.

Benefits from Study
of the Aggressive Body

Winnicott's views of aggression's roots in the body are valuable in several ways. First, retaining the notion of an aggressive drive is a valuable, if imprecise, step toward keeping the "psyche-soma" in view, to remind us that aggression is not mind or body but mind-body.[21] It helps us not minimize the importance and satisfaction of bodily experience during aggression and reminds us that its pleasureableness becomes seductive if denied. Further, Winnicott offers us an important distinction between an aggressive drive and a destructive instinct. This distinction leads to a refreshing addition to aggression theory: the focus is not only on our capacities for violence but also on the enlivening forces that reside in the psyche and can be marshaled for vital, constructive living. Violence is not sidestepped, but neither is research into the psychological capacities that could empower us to, for example, intervene in and diminish violence. Further, Winnicott's view that aggressive actions arise out of the interaction of constitution and environment supports us in shucking off the pessimistic and deterministic view of violence as instinctual: our behavior is "driven," but it is also at least somewhat malleable.

Winnicott is not alone in directing our attention to origins of aggressiveness in the body. As I noted in chapter 1, ongoing neurological, genetic, and hormonal research is investigating whether there is a cause of violent aggressiveness innate to the body. (Remember that aggression research in the biological sciences is focused on connections between aggression and violence, not vitality.) Most reliable at this point are results that show that some forms of organic pathology in the brain and other areas of the body can cause unprovoked violent behavior. Physiological research thus adds an important point to Winnicott's focus on the healthy essence of aggression's roots in the body. In the case of organic pathology, violent aggression may not be an expression of human life force or a response to threat but an involuntary reaction secondary to physiological processes. These organic problems can be present at birth or result from trauma.[22] In addition, while it appears that there is some relationship between sex hormones and harm-causing aggression, the nature of that relationship is in doubt and cannot be cited with certainty as an innate cause of aggressiveness. I also noted that genetics may play a role in the genesis of violent behavior, but again we have only limited and disputed findings.

We are far from proving any inborn physiological basis for the varied manifestations of violent aggression. The best assessment of the data at this point indicates that organic, genetic, and sexual characteristics constitute a potential for the development of violent tendencies, which may be actualized in response to environment and learning. But like Winnicott's attention to drives, research in the biological "first causes" of violent aggression helpfully keeps before us aggression's relationship to the body. It attends with unblinking diligence to the violence we often do with our aggression. Research that attends with such diligence to the physiology of vitality is just as needed.

Good-Enough Relationship and Everyday Failures: The Development of Healthy Aggressiveness

Aggression has a basis in our psychobiological existence, but its meanings and functions are revealed more profoundly in relationship with—and in mature dependency upon—others. What do we need to offer children in order to contain their violent impulses and also cultivate their constructive aggressiveness and encourage its appearance in our homes, churches, and neighborhoods? Surprisingly—and comfortingly—it is not perfection but rather the more modest tasks of *"good-enough" relationship* to adults, adults' *survival* of children's aggressiveness, and children's gradual exposure to the *everyday failures* endemic to living that play the most significant roles in children's development of healthy aggressiveness. If adults' aggression is distorted, we may find ourselves having to offer to adults—belatedly—similar relational qualities, if violence is to be transformed to nonviolent vitality. However, my focus in this chapter is on psychosocial processes in childhood that help actualize aggression's positive capacity. With childhood's foundational processes explored here, in chapter 5 I give attention to how we can care for distorted aggression in adults—ourselves and others.

Primary Preoccupation and Survival

In Winnicott's view, the first month or two after birth is a unique time in the development of aggression. While Winnicott assures the adults[23] caring for children that, for the vast majority of the child's life, they need not be perfect but good-enough, he does say that for the first weeks of a child's life a period of "primary preoccupation"[24] is the optimal condition for future growth. During this relatively brief period, the parents and other concerned adults should try to meet the child's needs as totally and quickly as possible. This temporary preoccupation is an expansion of the normal tendency for parents, especially, to become increasingly involved toward the end of pregnancy and at the time of birth in the emergence of this new life. As much as they can, parents should indulge themselves in this preoccupation—though they can do so only with the support of family and society—because this preoccupation best inaugurates "the psychological birth of the child."[25] While doctors and midwives attend to the physical delivery of the child, this period of preoccupation is the psychospiritual midwifery of the child and continues the process of easing the child out of the womb.

During the period of preoccupation, to the degree that children's energies are not exhausted in responding to impingements from outside, infants are freed to have their own preoccupation—with their new life in the world outside the womb. Children's needs are at first primarily physical but soon become emotional and intersubjective. Crucial aspects of healthy selfhood are begun. Having their needs met as completely as possible in these few weeks begins to build infants' confidence and get their sense of security off to a good start. Through loving attention, adults lend to babies "parts" of themselves, and those parts become internalized objects:[26] bits of the adults' goodness are "seeded" in the infant's internal world, psychological "graftings" that serve as starters for the "children's confidence in their own goodness." The care offered in this period lays the basis for ego integration, for the sense of "going on being."[27]

Infants experience their aggressiveness in this period, clinical observation indicates, as "raw" manifestations of the life force. One dimension of this aggressive experience is primarily intrapsychic. Postnatal life involves infants in new experiences of bodily needs and pleasure—hunger, feeding, elimination, touch. This new dimension of life outside the womb is embellished by fantasy—"imaginative elaboration of physical existence."[28] About the quality of this fantasy we must not be "sentimental," Winnicott cautions. We must assume that the vigor of the life force, as seen in the voraciousness of infants' eating and in the spontaneity of their movement, is imaginatively elaborated in infants' psychic life through images of devouring and attacking, what Winnicott calls "magical destruction."[29] Imagine this new world, from the infants' point of view: their hunger makes a bottle or breast appear; they close their eyes and people disappear. From the infants' point of view, object relations clinicians theorize, in an excited state their desire seems powerful enough to control, devour, and destroy. In these ways, the period of preoccupation gives infants a feeling of "omnipotence"—a sense of their own powerful agency.[30] This omnipotence later has to be modulated, as we will discuss. But it is necessary that this feeling of omnipotence get started because it is from experience of their power that later emerges children's (and adults') capacity to respond effectively to the impingements of the world that caring adults are, for these brief weeks, holding back. If awakened in childhood, this early sense of omnipotence can later be matured into the healthy self-respect that lies at the foundation of effective adult assertiveness. Without a core of childhood confidence in one's aggressiveness, an adult often relies upon an external veneer of omnipotence or some other form of excessive aggressiveness in order to be assertive at all.

As this discussion implies, infants' experience of aggressiveness in this period is conditioned not only by internal experience but also by discovery of the environment. At the most basic level, the exercise of aggressiveness teaches us that otherness exists. This is most concretely true for our newborns, who discover the world outside themselves when their thrashing legs and arms collide with people and things. Aggression is physical and emotional movement and initiative that brings us into contact with others. Thus, this aspect of aggressiveness leads children into the context of relationship, though infants may be unaware of this process. During this period, infants have only fledgling awareness of others as separate entities. The bottle, diaper, and loving embrace are inextricably tied up with infants' experience of self. In the mystifying—at least to an infant—first weeks of life, during this short period of preoccupation, adults give to infants a blessing if they enable infants to have the brief but soothing illusion that these factors are under their control.

The "relational" aggressiveness of infants and children may cause damage, even though young children do not intend—or even understand their capacity—to harm others. I remember vividly the Sunday morning coffee hour where I was introduced to a very young child being held in her mother's arms. As I leaned toward her, the child suddenly reached out and grabbed my nose. She giggled as she delightedly twisted it back and forth, oblivious to my pain. This is what Winnicott calls being "destructive by chance."[31] Like infants who bite their mothers while nursing or pull their grandfathers' beards while being held, this aggressiveness is an expression of excitement that is "pre-ruth," prior to the capacity to be ruthless or feel concern.[32] There is little evidence that an infant understands that "what he destroys when excited is the same as that which he values in quiet intervals between excitements."[33] Further, although the infant's aggressiveness may be experienced by others as destructive, there is insufficient ego integration at this period to impute to the infant intent to harm.[34] Quite the opposite is true, for the infant's impulsive gestures are excited and pleasurable ways of reaching out to these fascinating others just being discovered. These gestures are first signs of the object seeking that, according to object relations theory, motivates the human personality.[35] They are crude manifestations of the fusion of the erotic drive and life force: "Here is aggression as a part of love."[36] The social psychologist Marshall Segall calls these impulses "protoaggressions." They are not intentionally violent at this point, but they are prototypes of the energies and movements that will later be used for intentional harm-doing.[37]

Winnicott emphasizes repeatedly that during children's aggressive "attacks," it is crucial that caring adults around them survive and communicate their survival to the children through adult constancy. This survival of children's aggressiveness is critical not only during the period of primary preoccupation but throughout children's development. This is not to say that limits are not to be set on older children's violent aggressive actions. I will address the timing and value of limit-setting to the development of healthy aggressiveness shortly, when we consider the complementary value of parental "failures." For now our attention must be focused on something even more crucial to the development of nonviolent but vital young people and adults: young children need to learn deeply and experience viscerally that power—especially their own—is not as terrifyingly bad as it often seems to them.

To survive children's aggressiveness means that adults approach children's exploration of destructiveness as necessary for development of healthy agency, just as crawling must be learned before walking. To survive means that adults not impugn children's character for their mistakes in aggression, but help children practice the expression of aggression in safe and creative ways. To survive means that adults are not punitive or retaliatory, but allow themselves to be used in this way.[38] Indeed, because of the immense needs and raw aggressiveness of children, adults will likely *feel* used and even attacked, emotionally and sometimes physically. But it is critical that we communicate to children that we can and will survive their most powerful impulses, staying near to help them use constructively their vigorous emotions and bodies as much as to contain their impulses to do harm.

What is the cost if adults flee children's aggressiveness or become punitive and retaliatory in more direct ways? Among the lessons adults thus communicate to children are the following: they, too, might as well flee relationship to and responsibility for aggressiveness; they, too, ought to seek or expect isolation when feelings get strong; they, too, can rightly allow themselves to be overwhelmed and nonresponsive when violence rears its ugly head; they are powerful enough to drive away adults who love them.

Adults' ability to survive children's aggression cannot be assumed. As the prevalence of child abuse shows, and as I discuss later in this chapter, adults are frequently undone by an infant's aggressiveness and lash out. This is a sign of the adult's weakness, however, not the child's destructiveness. "Although destruction is the word I am using, this actual destruction belongs to the object's failure to survive. Without this failure, destruction remains potential."[39]

This "devotion" of surviving a child's aggressive impulses is difficult, and it gets harder as the child ages. The short period of preoccupation and the years of survival are more likely to be extended to children in cultures where extended families, neighborhoods, and communities help rear children, where one or two individuals are not left on their own to meet the many needs of a child.

The Values of Everyday Failures

One of the characteristics of Winnicott's theory that makes it so widely useful is that he understands how fleeting is the period in which any parent can protect a child from impingements, or should. Just when Winnicott's emphasis on survival threatens to overwhelm adults with responsibility, he introduces one of his theories' ambiguities: children do not need adult perfection in order to mature. Perfection in rearing children is problematic because adults, setting out to meet every need, inevitably end up trying to anticipate children's needs by reading their minds. Even if adults are correct, too much mind reading can be a disservice to children, whose process of reading their own minds, knowing their own needs, and voicing their own desires may be short-circuited. Aggressive energies—children's movement and vitality in the service of discovery of self, family, and community—thus lay dormant or are repressed to please adults.

Therefore, Winnicott urges families to allow themselves to move fairly quickly from the near-perfection of primary preoccupation into being good-enough.[40] We are good-enough in our engagements with developing children when we offer a loving combination of allowing their individual selves and their needs to emerge, meeting their needs, and gradually enabling them to meet their own needs on occasion. The younger the child, the more emphasis can be placed on "being there" for the child—physical holding, emotional mirroring, and so on. But as children grow, we ought not create the perception in children that the good things in life consist in always getting their needs met by other people. We must allow children to know—but not force it on them too soon—that the world does not exist for the satisfaction of any one individual's needs. Moreover, adults give children a gift when they allow children to discover early the pleasure that comes from occasionally taking on a challenge related to asserting or meeting their own needs and struggling successfully with that challenge. Similarly, adults gift children when they allow them to experience the pleasure that can come from choosing occasionally to moderate personal needs in deference to a larger whole of which they feel a part.

In this sense, children are owed learning from adults' everyday failures—not neglect or abuse but the normal limitations that go along with being human— tensions, delays, and disappointments that are not too traumatic and that come to an end.[41] As soon as young children show signs of being able to tolerate it— such as being able to console themselves when upset and to play alone—they should gradually be exposed to failures that are tolerable. Thus, the role of the loving others around the child is comprised by a delicate process of discernment: to know when and how to begin to introduce the amount of "opposition" necessary for the child's maturation, especially in relation to aggressiveness.[42]

Limit-setting is one important dimension of adults' valuable "failures." To set a limit on some behaviors is to "fail" to indulge children in risky actions because we also wish to "fail" to expose them to unnecessary danger—crossing streets between cars, wandering off with strangers, playing football too young, staying out too late, and so forth. As I noted above, when we set only necessary limits and set them lovingly, then limit-setting is one way to demonstrate to children that we have survived their destructiveness: we can "fail" to allow their aggressiveness to induce us to physically or emotionally withdraw or become punitive; instead we "hang in there," working with children to find a way that their aggressiveness can be expressed without hurting themselves or others.

Adults must have their own healthy aggressiveness to carry out this aspect of childrearing. That is, adults must be psychospiritually centered by an always-maturing consciousness regarding the strengths, vulnerabilities, and destructiveness within ourselves and our communities. From this point of view we can see that Winnicott's use of the word "failure" is satirical. When adults set limits on children not because of our normal limitations or because of the children's needs for guidance but because we feel like actual failures, it is precisely then that we are most likely really to fail children, not in the sense Winnicott intends but in unhelpful or even traumatic ways.

What is happening with the children in this process? As children continue to experience the primal union of aggressive and loving impulses—their life force-love, we could call it—the discovery of otherness gradually moves in the direction of the identification of the distinction between the Not-Me and Me. Physically and emotionally bumping about, they encounter "opposition," people and things they cannot move or control. They are confronted by frustrating and sometimes threatening delays in the meeting of their needs, even as they are becoming aware of their dependence on these uncontrollable others for their survival.

A further dimension of everyday failure comes from within, and these frustrations and threats adults will assuredly fail to fully prevent. Winnicott's description captures the shifting sands of the child's internal reality:

> The early stages of emotional development are full of potential conflict and disruption. The relation to external reality is not yet firmly rooted; the personality is not yet well integrated; primitive love has a destructive aim; and the small child has not yet learned to tolerate and cope with instincts.[43]

Frustration and threat are initially experienced internally and within the extended family. But if we think of slightly older children, then everyday failures come from a third location—the broader external environment. Consider all the worlds even young children might encounter—neighborhood, day care, playground, church, stores, and, a bit later, school. Through these normal exposures to the world beyond the child's own home, very young children begin to become aware at least of other children's aggressiveness, and probably of the inequities linked to difference, including class, race, gender, and religion.[44] Through television, the child is exposed less directly to many other worlds. Most children (and adults) spend many hours a day looking into the mirror of the television, being held by the atmosphere created in the image of an adult world riven with conflict, greed, and violence. (When it is not a steady diet, and when there are adults able and willing to help them reflect on it, some measure of this imagery may helpfully dramatize and assist children to work through the unavoidable existential tension that is a normal part of life.)

Additionally, as children age, many families must consciously prepare them for the threat they will find in the world—how the systemic and interpersonal destructiveness of forces like racism, sexism, sexual violence, religious intolerance, and classism will affect the children. This sense of environmental failure is so pervasive, so everyday, for people of color in the United States that psychologist Thomas Parham has developed a model of identity development for African Americans centered on the metaphor of a hurricane.[45] These threats and failures in the world outside the home not infrequently lead children to conflicts in their own aggressive behavior. As I will soon address, however, such conflicts are much less likely to destroy children if adults around them have taught them—by example—how to survive, and thrive, in the midst of aggressiveness.

Children's Response to Everyday Failures and Threats

What are these internal and external "failures" like for children? If children encounter these everyday failures while being "held" in a good-enough environment, they eventually weather and grow in the midst of the creative tension. But initially, when they glimpse their lack of control and the potential threat, they test and protest aggressively.

> What is the normal child like? Does he just eat and grow and smile sweetly? No, that is not what he is like. A normal child, if he has

confidence in father and mother, pulls out all the stops. In the course of time he tries out his power to disrupt, to destroy, to frighten, to wear down, to waste, to wrangle and to appropriate.[46]

This is the second meaning Winnicott imputes to aggression: it is a response to *actual and perceived* frustration and threat. The sense of frustration and threat registers, of course, not only emotionally but also physically. Laboratory research in the physiology of aggression shows that when a threat is sensed, the complex limbic system sets in motion a bodily reaction that radiates out from the brain to include increased heart rate, goose bumps on the skin, and agitation in arms and legs. Given that adults often feel terrified by their own biological reactions to stress and fear, it is likely that infants also feel threatened by their internal reactions to the sense of threat outside.

These physiological reactions accentuate psychological dynamics set in motion by frustration and the sense of threat. Even simple, everyday failures frustrate children's object seeking, and children (and, later object-seeking adults) respond with "destructive" aggression to this felt deprivation and absence of response.[47] As I noted earlier, the need to respond to frustration and threat undermines conscious experience of the kinship of love and aggression. Aggression and love now likely feel split, no longer fused and able to temper each other. Moreover, their rage reactions to the threat may seem to the children able to destroy the very being upon whom children know they depend for survival. The internalized good objects, seeded in the first weeks and growing, may not be strong enough to help children successfully withstand the barrage of these bad feelings within. Children may psychologically split the objects, wanting to protect their "good parts" from being tainted by their "bad parts." Projective mechanisms may also send the bad outside: Children may blame the frustrating objects "outside" for this whirlwind of feeling, not able to tolerate their own thinking and feeling.

Thus, physically and psychologically, in response to internal and external frustration and threat, children "pull out all the stops" in terms of destructiveness, as Winnicott puts it. Ironically, in doing so they are looking for "a framework," for "a circle of love and strength" that, even though not perfect, will help them navigate the uncertain atmosphere inside and outside.[48] Children and the adults around them enter into an extremely critical phase in terms of aggression. As in the period of preoccupation, it is crucial that the family survive this more intense round of aggressiveness and that they not use their own aggressiveness to retaliate.

Though the family's work is about the same, its meaning to children is quite different and enormously formative. Given the good start we have been describing, children have a growing amount of ego integration, and now, when their parents and others survive their destructiveness, several essential processes are set in motion. They have the capacity to notice that others have survived their impulses to destroy them, and this teaches them that their aggression has limits and is not categorically to be feared. This rescues it from repression. Further, when they set out to destroy the object and it survives, this engages them in the "placing of the object outside the area of [their] omnipotent control."[49] They are beginning to know that their "objects"—both people and things—are not pawns in an inner world but subjects in their own right. Others are more real to them, "not just a bundle of projections."

These dynamics are the foundation for building up in children the very positive "capacity to feel concern," or what is more negatively called *guilt*.[50] Children begin to have the capacity to recognize that the one against whom they direct their rage is also the one toward whom they feel love. For the first time, they are able to experience regret for their destructive desires. Now, and only now, can children care about the fate of their objects, feel appropriate remorse for their actions, and be motivated and have the opportunity to take responsibility for their actions through constructive aggressiveness. Thus, only through experience of situations in which their destructive aggressiveness is lovingly survived can they have the capacity or desire for regret or "reparation," the desire to set things right, to repair what they have damaged.[51] Moreover, it is at this point of genuine remorse for aggressiveness that a child begins to build *consciousness* of the kinship of love and aggression that was there all the time but had not yet made its way into experience. Sustained consciousness of the kinship of love and aggression, and the capacity to act on the basis of it, is an achievement of maturity. Here, however, it gets its start. These enormous emotional accomplishments explain why children who receive primary preoccupation and adult survival of their aggressiveness have the capacity to show more contrition and compassion than many adults.

Finally, though it has been thought that reality and its frustrations have created aggressiveness, this process suggests the opposite, that aggressiveness creates reality. The "destructive drive" creates the quality of externality."[52] Now, instead of simply relating "as an isolate," unconscious and in violation of the object's integrity, the object can be more maturely used. Use of an object, as Winnicott details it, is not exploitation. The survival and new reality of the object create a safe enough environment in which children (and adults) can keep on growing into a constructive use of their destructiveness, *in fantasy*. Winnicott suggests the child's inner process:

> The subject [child] says to the object: "I destroyed you," and the object is there to receive the communication. From now on the subject says, "Hullo object!" "I destroyed you." "I love you." "You have value for me because of your survival of my destruction of you." "While I am loving you I am all the time destroying you in (unconscious) *fantasy*." Here fantasy begins for the individual. The subject can now *use* the object that has survived.[53]

Note the enormous gains of this period. When children are given the opportunity to pull out all the stops in aggression, set out to destroy an object, and be confronted with the fact that it survives, they are on their way to learning many things: constructive use of aggressiveness, the reality and value of others, how to relate to others as subjects in their own right, the feeling of concern when their aggressiveness does cause harm, their capacity to use their aggression to set things right, and the richness of fantasy for psychospiritual growth. No wonder Winnicott observes understatedly that within children "there could be said to be joy at the object's survival."[54]

Potential Space,
Lifelong Learning, and Aggression

Of course, the deep learning of these lessons is an ongoing task, occupying adults as well as children. Children and adults both need room to practice navigating the ambiguities of vitality and violence, of good-enough survival, and too-much failure. Thus there is another aspect of the "framework" and "circle of love and strength" in which constructive aggression is learned. Winnicott calls this *potential space*. Potential space is a part of a facilitating environment, created first between the growing child and loving adults and later between adults and their cultural symbols and activities.[55] Potential space is not fully either internal or external. It is "an intermediate area of *experiencing*," important for the "perpetual human task of keeping inner and outer reality separate yet interrelated."[56] It is play and creativity utilized in the creation of what Winnicott calls "transitional objects" and "transitional phenomena": areas of experience that exist internally, externally, and at the border between.[57] Through the illusory experience of play and creativity, transitional objects and phenomena are endowed with characteristics that assist us in navigating the transitions between inner and outer reality, between Me and Not-Me, and between childhood omnipotence and adult capability. In contrast to reality's constant challenges to omnipotence, playful illusion ought not be challenged, lest it lose its capacity to bridge reality and fantasy.

In potential space, children and adults are given a safe-enough container in which to reveal aggression and play around with it. Like other transformative elements in potential space, healthy aggressiveness is, paradoxically, both found and created. In the aggressiveness of play, spontaneity emerges. Winnicott observes that healthy aggressiveness is very much akin to spontaneity[58] and that "the spontaneous gesture is the True Self in action."[59] In the spontaneity of play can emerge the aggressiveness that enables a person, over time, to "repudiate the shell and become the core."[60] Aggressiveness—including destructive fantasy—is also often a part of the creativity of play.[61] Aggressiveness in the creative fantasy of play assists children and adults to avoid too much compliance, which is death to the true self.[62] Through playing around with one's power in the supportive relationship of potential space, the omnipotence of childhood can be shaped toward the capacity for healthy assertion and sense of agency in community,[63] so central to effective adulthood, where aggression manifests as the ability to reach out to, connect with, and craft compromises with others.

In aggressive play, children and adults can also learn the actual effects of destructiveness, both its limits and its real damages. The experience that some aggressiveness is survivable prevents its complete repression. The experience that some aggressiveness causes real wounds exposes us to the opportunity to feel authentic regret and concern for another. If it is experienced before we can inflict fatal wounds, there is also opportunity to learn that the destructiveness of aggression can often be repaired.[64] Indeed, reparation for one's destructive aggression can be itself an experience of powerful agency.

One final insight about potential space comes from social learning theories of aggression. In the processes we have been describing, family and others are teaching children cultural meanings and social mores in aggression, even when we are unaware of it or want to subvert socialization processes. Families and teachers are major agents in the socialization processes that create the "social representations" that direct our dealings with aggression. Social representations are the "everyday theories" (note the plural) we hold about aggression, the pictures and interpretations we have of where aggression comes from and what aggression means and accomplishes. Our thinking, feeling, and behavior in regard to aggression are significantly shaped, often unconsciously, by the social representations we have of aggression. These representations of aggression are communal, not personal; they are built through our interactions with and observations of parents and other authority figures, siblings and friends, education and play, government and religious bodies, media and art.[65]

Social learning theories of aggression emphasize that violently aggressive behavior is often imitative, learned early in life from admired or powerful adults in a child's life.[66] But in potential space, the loving network around the child has the opportunity to teach new social representations of aggression, for example, constructively aggressive nonviolence. The ways in which we respond to children's aggressiveness teach them at least two things: how to express aggressiveness and how to respond to others' aggressiveness. The creativity of potential space provides adults opportunity to practice being for children nonretaliatory, nonpunitive models in response to necessary aggression. We can model for children the discernment between aggressiveness that is not destructive (though perhaps challenging to others) and violent aggressiveness.

Winnicott emphasizes that, in potential space, adults are inviting out the child's true self. This is more partially and radically true than he seems aware. In transitional space, two things can be happening. Adults are inculcating the child to social values in aggression by teaching the rules of aggression, both necessary and unnecessary (for example, "share your toys," "big boys don't cry," "nice girls don't yell"), and in so doing they risk teaching too much compliance and false self values. In contrast, if they are intentional about it, in potential space, adults can help children be themselves in the face of the rules, not simply comply and completely repress their aggressiveness.[67] For example, during play with children, adults ought to focus not only on discouraging children from forming weapons with their toys but also on helping children play around with nondangerous but affirming and strong ways of expressing their aggression. We are not simply controlled by rules, as postmodern theory would have us believe.[68] Potential space can help us transform social representations of aggression.

Trauma, Domination-Subjugation, and Distorted Aggression

Psychoanalyst Karen Horney criticized Sigmund Freud for positing a human instinct of destructiveness. She said he erroneously did so because he did not take into sufficient account that there are reasons in the environment to be destructive.[69] Violence is a reaction to the violence in psychic, relational, and social environments, she countered, not evidence of an instinctual destructiveness, essential to human nature. She defended her claim with this metaphor: "If a tree, because of storms, too little sun or too poor soil, becomes warped and crooked, you would not call this its essential nature."[70]

In this section, we examine some of the environmental conditions that cause aggression to become "warped and crooked." The causes of violence are multiple, and our efforts to decrease violent aggressiveness must be multifaceted. But I argue that a primary cause of distorted aggression—both violence and lack of vitality—is the trauma of personal and social relationships of domination and subjugation that suppress constructive aggressiveness in individuals and in groups. We can say this another way: aggression is distorted when a person or group feels that more constructive expressions of aggression are threatened or made pointless by domination.[71] (This is not to say that adults are not responsible for the effects of distortion in their aggression; we are talking here only about causes.) The threat against aggressiveness may be immediate and obvious to everyone, or it may be cumulative, historical, and perhaps invisible to onlookers.

My approach to the study of distorted aggression is akin to social interactionist theory, which studies harm-doing actions on the basis of four principles. First, destructive aggressiveness is interpreted as instrumental, as a means to achieving certain values or goals. Second, destructive aggression is seen as the normal consequence of conflict in human relations, not as the compulsory, outward expression of a continuous inner drive. Third, because situational and interpersonal factors are seen as important generators of destructive aggression, social interactionist theory considers the participation of provocateurs as well as that of the identified aggressor. Fourth, aggressors' phenomenology, their values and perceptions, are considered important factors in the assessment of aggression.[72]

Failure to
Survive Aggression: Three Forms

As crucial as everyday failures are to maturation, too much failure too soon is traumatic. From Winnicott's point of view, distorted aggression is a sign of too much failure in a person's early and later environments, and thus, traumatic wounding. More specifically, either too much compliance or too much destructiveness in a person's way of living suggests that at some early point no significant person was able to survive that destructiveness and that the person has not yet found later "survivors" sufficient to repair the early wounds. Winnicott is thinking about childhood, but we can apply this idea more widely. Environment is more than parents or family or even neighborhood. Thus, another location for the failure to survive aggression comes from the broader environment—education, religion, politics, economics. Even from the beginning of a child's life, these broader environmental problems play a role because they impinge upon members of the child's family, who in turn are faced with trying to survive the child's destructiveness. We consider in the following discussion not only traumatic interpersonal failures, but also in what ways the broader environment fails to survive sufficiently a child's aggressiveness and fails to remediate that failure with adults. Interpersonal and social failure to survive aggression takes at least three forms.

One form of failure to survive destructiveness is neglect of it. Here, nothing is given to children to help them deal with their aggressiveness. Significant adults may neglect destructive children by actually abandoning them or by leaving them emotionally. (I am not talking about the often helpful response of not *over*reacting to a child's destructiveness. Rather, I am talking about giving the distressed child nothing back affectively except emotional flatness.) Adults may also abandon children's aggressiveness by romanticizing them and not taking their aggressiveness seriously. I mentioned in the previous section Winnicott's admonition not to be sentimental about a child's aggressiveness—treating it as cute or an object of ridicule. Sentimentality is "withering" to the child at first, and aggression that, if taken seriously, would have been constructively expressed, will likely be expressed more destructively.[73]

In the environment beyond the home, this failure to survive aggressiveness through neglect can be seen in several examples. One example of the failure to survive one another's aggressiveness is found in the avoidance of conflict or its resolution. Sometimes people actually walk away from an argument. More common, however, are situations where we simply refuse to acknowledge conflicts. Another example in day-to-day life is found in lack of responsiveness to complaints about products or services, in which legitimate problems are met with studied indifference. An example of failure to survive aggressiveness through sentimentalizing can be seen in situations where women's aggressiveness is derided and minimized as "cute." In these situations, attempts to express aggressiveness in direct and constructive ways are minimized, ignored, and trivialized.

Another way that the environment fails to survive destructiveness is by invasion. Here, children are given too much "help," and their agency is overwhelmed. Concerned adults so adapt to children's needs that the children have no opportunity to fend for themselves.[74] This failure is often not seen as such, since it looks like devotion to a child. But too much help—perhaps due to adults' anxiety about their own aggression and lack of trust in children's ability to survive or modulate their own aggressiveness—fills in the space where children's initiative and destructiveness should be. In the broader environment, an example of failure by invasion is seen in workplaces where supervisors observe and control employees too closely; where creativity and fruitful mistakes could be, such supervisors fill in the space with their own ideas and judgments, breeding in employees dull resignation and simmering resentment.

Finally and probably most commonly, failure to survive children's destructiveness can take the form of retaliation and punitive squelching that have as their goal children's acquiescence. This clamping down is sometimes physical. But often—and arguably more damaging—emotional violence is aimed at destroying manifestations of children's aggressiveness. Swiss analyst Alice Miller's notion of the "vicious circle of contempt" serves us well in trying to elucidate the nature of this kind of control of aggressiveness.[75] The parents or others in the children's environment react to children's aggressiveness with cruelty and show a lack of empathy for children's struggles and relative helplessness. This form of failure is perpetuated by childrearing traditions wherein parents and other adults are given absolute power over children. The power is frequently used to "discipline" children's aggressiveness, which too often means trying to rub out their aggressiveness and shatters children's regard for self and other. Adults respond to children's aggressiveness contemptuously because, when they were children, adults dealt with their aggressiveness contemptuously. Robbed of aggressiveness, the adults are left feeling weak, and they anesthetize themselves against their feelings of powerlessness by wielding contempt over children. "Contempt is the weapon of the weak."[76] The adult steals from the child's aggressiveness.

The vicious circle continues when the children now being humiliated take their places as "heads" of children over whom they have the power to exercise contemptuous discipline. Examples of the vicious circle of contempt and its interrelationship with aggressiveness abound in the broader external environment. One clear example is found in academia, where professors not infrequently train their students with techniques of contemptuous critique and hazing handed down to them from their professors. Today's students too often become tomorrow's contemptuous ministers, physicians, professors, lawyers, and other professionals.

Aggression Distorted: Pathological Introversion and the Antisocial Tendency

Adults' failure to survive children's destructiveness suppresses children's constructive aggression. Because constructive aggression is dependent upon healthy relationship, if no one is there to receive it, children's constructive aggression initially goes underground. What happens next is complex and varies from child to child, of course. But Winnicott's ideas help us see trees and not just forest. Suppression of constructive aggression is likely to result in one, or a combination, of two general trends—what Winnicott calls *pathological introversion* and the *antisocial tendency*. In these two trends, and in the three more specific wounds we will discuss shortly, we will see the particular contribution of social cognitive approaches to aggression theory: children learn violent aggression not only through mimicking the violent behavior of people around them; they sometimes learn violent behavior as complement to the interpretations they place on the ostensibly nonaggressive, but nonetheless violent and traumatizing, behavior they see in adults. Passive parents may say, for example, that they suppress aggression in themselves and their children out of love, but the children may detect some other motivation—jealousy, for example—and offer to their parents these distortions in aggression in return.

Pathological Introversion

Left alone with their destructiveness and terrified, some children engage in psychological splitting. They project destructiveness outside, concentrate their good feelings inside—including all the goodness associated with their aggressiveness, and then retreat to that inner world, withdrawn—"pathologically introverted."[77] Children accomplish self-defense, increased safety, and retaliation ("robbing" the other by going away) through withdrawal. From a social learning perspective, these children have learned to handle aggression through imitating the adults who responded to their aggression with neglect and retreat.

To protect the true self, these children construct a submissive false self through which they operate in the world—"a shop-window or out-turned half"—while the true self "containing all the spontaneity is kept secret and is all the time involved in hidden relationships to idealized fantasy objects."[78] Often, however, these children become so involved in the compliance, so identified with the false self, that the true self feels "un-get-at-able," and they lose touch with both inner and outer worlds.[79] Moreover, because their destructiveness is projected onto others, these children may feel they have no adequate defense against the destructiveness of others and allow themselves to be attacked and diminished without defending themselves or even setting limits. In this extremity, the false self's passive compliance may annihilate the true self. Here we see the dynamic identified by social cognitive theory: The pathologically introverted child has interpreted adults' ostensibly nonviolent, nonaggressive neglect and retreat as an indication that the true self is not deserving of protection and perhaps not of survival. The child does not simply mimic the adult, neglect the aggressiveness of the true self, and risk his or her exposure, but goes further, by giving away (projecting) aggressiveness and thus assuring that she or he is completely vulnerable to destruction.

Thus, it cannot be said that pathological introversion is not violent. The original goal was self-protection, but the end result is often self-destruction. Though rarely acknowledged, especially by compliant people, compliance is often the "upper side" of destructiveness. Winnicott puts it bluntly:

> In a study of the psychology of aggression a severe strain is imposed on the student, for the following reason. In a total psychology, being-stolen-from is the same as stealing, and is equally aggressive. Being weak is as aggressive as the attack of the strong on the weak. Murder and suicide are fundamentally the same thing. . . .
>
> These considerations are painful, because they draw attention to dissociations that are hidden in current social acceptance.[80]

Antisocial Tendency

Left alone with their destructiveness and terrified, other people identify themselves with their destructiveness and use it to "shake society up till it provides cover."[81] The delinquency associated with the antisocial strategy may be more problematic for society than too much compliance. But Winnicott emphasizes the costs of compliance to the individual child. In the first place, as Winnicott puts it, "it is better to exist in prison than to become annihilated in meaningless compliance."[82] Further, persons who choose the compliant strategy do not know that the failure came from the environment. They turn inward, are not looking for anyone to help them repair the damage. They have given up hope.

By contrast, in the behaviors of "delinquency," children show that they know that it was the environment that failed, and these children have not yet given up hope that they might find something in the environment that would replace the goodness inside that was lost.[83] This indicates a level of ego maturity that is not necessarily present in people who are too compliant. (In this sense, it is pathological introversion that is literally antisocial.) In the antisocial strategy, the person feels real only when being destructive.[84] The violence in this strategy is easily identified. It is directed against the environment that failed. The antisocial tendency results in part from a lack of (conscious) fusion of the aggressive and erotic drives.[85] The false self created in this strategy faces the world as a dominator, in order to protect the true self. From a social learning perspective, such children have learned to handle aggression through imitating the adults who responded to their aggression with invasion and retaliation. Social cognitive theory underlines the hopeful aspect of the antisocial tendency: the child has, correctly, interpreted the adults' violent retaliation as misdirected.

In both pathological introversion and the antisocial tendency, the violence is not a matter of emotion or psychology only. The physiological aspects of aggression mentioned in chapter 1 remind us to consider what innate and environmental conditions may be playing a role in a child's or adult's violence. The affective reactions caused by the trauma of domination and subjugation are always interacting with powerful bodily and environmental factors.

Distorted Aggression's Wounds

Underlying and contributing to these two general trends in distorted aggression are more specific wounds. There are a number of ways that we could conceptualize the damage done, but consider these three: failure of connection, injury to or inability to get started in ego strength, and, narcissistic injury.

If, as Winnicott argues, aggression establishes externality, then the failure to survive aggression in any of the ways previously discussed represses the very emotional terrain in which one person finds another. It follows that the suppression of aggressiveness leads to some failure of connection. If children's destructiveness is intolerable to the adults around them and adults sidestep it or in more cruel ways prevent its appearance, adults save themselves difficulty only in the short run. Children whose aggressiveness is impinged upon in this way develop other problems. The adults see only that they are setting limits on the destructiveness and usually do not recognize that in the destructiveness is also children's love. Children's violence will likely increase because of adults' failure to connect lovingly in the presence of aggression.[86] As psychoanalyst Harry Guntrip puts it, "Hate is love grown angry because of rejection."[87]

This is not psychotherapeutic observation only. Laboratory research shows that failure to establish appropriate affectional bonds is a primary cause of violence. This includes, though it is not limited to, the deprivation of sensory and physical pleasure, which could be gained through aggressive activity.[88] Widespread failure of adults to survive girls' aggressiveness may well explain why one of the few forms of relational connection in which many women are not proficient is constructive aggressiveness. That boys' aggressiveness is more often survived and even nurtured may well explain why constructive aggressiveness is one form of relational connection with which many men have a fair degree of facility. This twist in gender stereotypes is one of the main topics of chapter 4.

Aggressiveness plays a role in the development of ego strength. Consciousness of the kinship of erotic and aggressive energies imparts a sense of the integration so central to ego strength. Further, Winnicott suggests that suppression of aggression, since it is so physiologically significant, suppresses body-needs, and it is out of body-needs that ego-needs develop. Thus, if the suppression of aggression happens early in the child's development, it could prevent or delay even the start of ego maturation. Deprivation (as contrasted to smaller privations), like that associated with the suppression of aggressiveness, causes breakdown of ego defenses.[89] In such a situation, reacting to the impingements of an environment distressed by its aggressiveness could present the threat of annihilation to the child's psyche.[90] If the suppression of aggressiveness takes the form of neglectful withdrawal by significant adults, then the child is deprived of ego-relatedness with significant adults in the realm of aggression, and they fail to be available to lend to the child bits of their ego strength in relation to the tolerance of aggression. Moments of ego-relatedness are the building blocks of ego strength, and their absence, especially where they concern aggressiveness, threatens to leave the child weak—undernourished, so to speak. Loss of aggression drains energy from the ego—it is a loss of ego spontaneity.[91] On the one hand, the lack of ego strength might interfere with the capacity to play around with omnipotence in fantasy and thus leave a person without a sufficient sense of agency and creativity. On the other hand, the lack of ego-strength can lead to exacerbated anxiety and a sense of helplessness. Destructive aggressiveness might then be rallied by the false self as a defense; Guntrip saw aggressive destructiveness as a veneer covering a fundamental lack of ego-strength.[92]

A third kind of woundedness that might result from the suppression of aggressiveness is narcissistic injury. The work of psychoanalyst Heinz Kohut is helpful here. For Kohut, nondestructive aggression is the foundation out of which develops the assertiveness of the part of the self he calls the "grandiose-exhibitionistic self."[93] Despite the negative associations we might have to a self so labeled, its name is appropriate because it refers to the self's ambitions and goals and to the immense assertion that must be part of the self to realize its enormous potential. (Its bravado can be kept in reasonable bounds by another aspect of the self, the "idealized parent imago," if appropriate values are inculcated from parents.[94]) These positive contributions of the aggressive, grandiose-exhibitionistic self are essential for building up a healthy sense of self-esteem, or what Kohut calls "healthy narcissism."[95] In Kohut's theory, narcissism is not essentially negative and is not necessarily excessive self-regard or the inability to love others. Rather, a healthy amount of narcissism or confidence in oneself is essential for effective living. The contribution of parents and other loving adults around children is to show empathy toward these aggressive expressions. The adults avoid retaliation and instead offer to children understanding of their inner experience, without abandoning the role of responsible adult.

If aggression is suppressed by the adults with whom a child relates most closely, the grandiose-exhibitionistic self is severely hampered in its job of energizing the total self for positive living. More seriously, because of this impeding of the grandiose-exhibitionistic self, the narcissism of the developing self is wounded. A major source of self-esteem is cut off in the suppression of aggression. Destructive aggression is likely to appear as a "disintegration product" of the failure of empathy.[96] More exactly, destructive aggression is likely to be expressed in the form of rage reactions, in response to wounded narcissism. The angry reaction is so strong because the injury is so serious. Adults' lack of empathy for the child's "grandiose" self leads to suppression of aggressiveness by the developing self, without which there is no fuel for basic narcissism, all of which threaten the self's cohesiveness. The distortions of aggression in narcissistic rage reactions are unforgettable once experienced. A self deeply weakened from lack of healthy narcissism finds its control through the unconscious subterfuge of forcing others into tightly prescribed roles on its inner stage. The slightest deviation from their appointed functions can result in an outpouring of hate and fury.[97]

We have traced aggression's transformations from the initial vitality of the life force, into the raw aggression of early love, and through the aggressive inventions of potential space. We have considered the costs when adults cannot survive children's aggression, the costs of introversion, antisociality, unrelatedness, ego-deficiency, and wounded narcissism. What can theological reflection add to our understanding of this complex human reality? In the next chapter, we turn to this question.

3

Toward a Theology of Aggression

Do not lag in zeal, be ardent in spirit, serve the Lord.
—Romans 12:11

Within [the] area of legitimate and anxiety-free expression of aggression
lies an important dynamic force for the future vitality of Christian life and
experience.

—William W. Meissner,
"Toward a Theology of Human Aggression"

IN A 1971 ARTICLE, Jesuit priest and psychiatrist William W.
Meissner observed the lack of formal Christian theological reflection
on aggression. Meissner speculated that this omission was based on
an assumption that aggression is the origin of the human capacity
to hate and that since "hate and the Christian life must be thought
of as antithetical," then "aggression and theology would have little
to do with each other."[1] Meissner did not comment on the wishful
thinking embedded in such a conclusion. He did observe that this
omission is a violation of the fundamental methodological principle
that, to be consequential and pertinent, theology must reflect on
all—not part—of the most profound roots of human nature and concern.[2] He set out some tentative theological observations about aggression and observed that because the theological tradition has not
"come to grips" with aggression, "the mentality of the Christian community is such that the expression of any aggression has become
overladen with a burden of restraint and suppression and excessive
guilt."[3] He concluded with an expression of hope for more theological dialogue about this potent human experience.

The situation has changed little since the publication of Meissner's
article. This is regrettable, in light of the complex mixture of danger

and promise that confronts us in human aggressiveness. We need theological reflection to guide us through the maze of possibilities presented by aggression. In this chapter, I explore how theological discussion illuminates the ambiguity and relationality of aggression and suggest principles by which aggression might be utilized in ethical ways. While we find little explicit discussion of aggression in theological literature, I argue that there is extensive indirect reference to aggression through which we can discern theological positions on its nature and dynamics. Within the vast project of developing a theology of aggression, the totality of which is beyond the scope of this book, I have chosen four broad theological themes for exploration in relation to the ambiguity and relationality of aggression: creation, power, liberation, and ethics. Four main claims regarding these themes frame our reflections. First, I argue that aggression is an aspect of our createdness, sacred in its essence and also available for our misuse. Second, aggression is an ambiguous and relational form of human power. Third, aggression is a double-edged tool in liberative resistance of oppression and in the building of just relationships. Finally, aggression's ambiguity and relationality require some reformulation of the ethical standards with which Christianity has traditionally approached human aggressiveness.

Aggression and
Theologies of Creation

The opening pages of the biblical narrative suggest the "given-ness" of power as an aspect of the human condition. In the first of the creation stories recorded, the initial thing we learn about the earthcreatures is that they are made in the image of an awesomely powerful God and given dominion over "every creeping thing." Through such a beginning, issues relating to the proper use of that power—but no suggestion that its forfeiture is possible—are established as central themes in any adequate theological anthropology. We will examine the proper use of power and, more exactly, its relation to aggression, shortly.

For now, our attention is focused on three other matters suggested by the creation narrative. First, power is an inherent aspect of the human condition. Made in the image of a God who has just created the heavens and the earth and then given dominion over God's tour de force, humanity comes into existence through and with power. "Being is saturated with power inevitably."[4] Like the other aspects of the creation project, God judges this piece of work "good." This assessment of power's goodness is made prior to particular employments of power and simply in the context of its creation. That power exists as part of the created order, God judges good. As the second version of the creation story makes clear, there are both free and restricted employments of power (Gen. 2:16–17). But the essential nature of power is "good"—sacred, we can imply.

As one form of power, it can be argued that aggression is part of our createdness and its stewardship is entrusted to us by the Creator. We are endowed
from birth with the significant initiative, assertion, enterprise, and boldness by
which we have defined aggression. Aggressiveness is a "basic dimension of our
creatureliness."[5] Moreover, our aggressiveness is not rebellious or harmful simply in its existence, though it may become so in specific employments. As part
of creation, aggression has potential for goodness and grace as well as for sin
and evil. Indeed, it would be a characterization opposite that of the creation
narrative to hold that aggressive power or aggressive behavior are "bad,"
merely because they exist. We cannot assess the value of our aggressive power
without examining the context in which we use it and the effects our aggression causes. Rather, we must wrestle with the sobering and challenging notion
that "aggression participates in the goodness of creation."[6] Created in the image of a powerful God, we are bequeathed in aggression a vigorous aliveness
and the capacity to be effectual.

Second, the first chapters of the biblical narrative quickly make clear another
truth about power. Though the existence of power is judged good, power becomes immediately and profoundly ambiguous in the living out of it. However
essential and positive power is as an aspect of human nature, it becomes a confounding mixture of bane and blessing as soon as it is exercised in the context
of relationship. The second creation story dramatizes this. The story tells us that
the first exercise of human power is to eat of the tree of the knowledge of good
and evil. On the one hand, this action is taken in contradiction to the com-
mands of God and artistically introduces human culpability in, and shame for,
the embodiment of evil. On the other hand, it becomes the first occasion in the
story when one human being shares with another the enjoyment of power: "So
when the woman saw that the tree was good for food, and that it was a de-
light to the eyes, and that the tree was to be desired to make one wise, she
took of its fruit and ate; and she also gave some to her husband . . . " (Gen.
3:6). Power comes from God and yet, for the sake of human freedom, some
power is relinquished by God as well to the realm of human relationship and
limitation, imparting to power an inherent, unresolvable ambiguity.[7] Because
we are created into relationship, the nascent goodness of power is hardly experienced, so quickly does its multivalency come to the fore. Thus our "elemental powers" are more often than not tragic: they are for us "vital integral
dimensions of life," and at the same time they are also caught in "elemental
conflicts" with powers in other dimensions—the needs of other people and the
cosmos, the demands of faithfulness to God.[8]

We see here articulated theologically the complexity in newborn aggression
Winnicott tries to describe psychologically. The aggressiveness in the new being—infant or 'adam—is essential energy that gives life, its destructiveness only
potential. But because babies and earthcreatures are born into a profound
interdependency, that potential for destructiveness is immediately at issue. We
can interpret the woman's decision to eat of the tree as the first significant

initiative, assertion, enterprise, and boldness in the human story. Unfortunately, her aggressiveness is undertaken in naive trust in the serpent's assurances that knowledge of good and evil would not lead to death. But she does encounter a kind of death, a death of innocence. Her aggressivity is fundamentally tragic. Its existence in her is all at once "elemental power" and "elemental conflict," a flirtation with evil. There is no longer any simple answer to the question of aggression's value, only a "tragic heuristic,"[9] in which we must always be questioning, questioning, questioning the morality of our aggressive actions. It is harder to use aggression wisely than to forfeit it. About this Genesis creation account, feminist theologian Carter Heyward says,

> The moral of the story is that it is easier to be ignorant, harder to know; easier to be passive, harder to be aggressive; easier to comply with external authority, harder to claim one's own power; easier to be created, harder to create. It is much easier to be established in the garden we have learned to call Paradise than to pick up our beds and walk into the world.[10]

Unexpectedly, amid the complexity, we find some relief in this. It was impossible anyway, and exhausting, always having to be right (and, consequently, too often righteous) in our expression of aggression. We are left with the humbler task of naming and acting in the face of aggression's ambiguity. Perhaps we have not so much been cast out of paradise as aggressively escaped its simplistic renderings of human power.[11]

Finally, the creation story suggests that the relationality of power provides a guideline through the maze of relativity that might otherwise be created by power's ambiguity. Douglas John Hall's exposition of the meaning of being created in the image of God is helpful here.[12] Hall suggests that the idea of being made in the likeness of God suggests "the ontology of communion" more than it concerns the imparting to human beings of specific qualities; that is, the specific qualities of our being are "secondary considerations" and "means . . . to the end that we may be able to enter into the rather complex constellation of relationships for which we are intended."[13] We are made for relationship, and the power with which we are entrusted—"dominion"—is for the strengthening of our relational context, not an end in itself. We return to the meaning of dominion later.

For now, I want to emphasize that the creation myth artistically makes a point about power very similar to one made by Winnicott about aggression—that its most important and nondestructive function is in furthering relationality. Hall's identification of the functional alliance between power and relationality reiterates the need to consciously cultivate a close relationship between love and aggression. Aggression enlivens us for the purpose of transporting us to and discovering actual otherness, we can infer from Hall, so that our relations with others are not solipsistic but move us into the rich space between us and others. If being made in the image of God is a call to relationality, then it is also a call to use all the power given us in aggression for developing not simply "doing" (as aggression is often caricatured) or "being" (where aggression is often wrongly assumed to be absent) but—as Hall calls it—"being-with" God, neighbors, and creation.[14] Being-with is a proactive living-out of the ontology of communion—we refuse to kowtow to individualistic images, values, or goals but instead stubbornly do the day-to-day work of linking ourselves to others.[15] A world of being-with would be "a world in which reality is discovered in reciprocity."[16]

Hall makes specific a point that is allowed for but never brought into the center of Winnicott's theory: *Being-with others* means relationship not only with human others but also with nature and God. From a depth psychological point of view, however, we need also to expand Hall's formulations by one dimension—the pleasure and responsibility of being-with ourselves. Thus, that our aggressive power is created in the image of God means that our aggressiveness is intended for being-with ourselves, others, nature, and God. Though being-with others often does involve the honest exploration of differences, the creation myth reminds us that aggressive power is not given to us for the purposes of isolation, judgmentalism, or attack. But this is easy to say and hard to do. Power's function for relationship may be given at creation but must be carefully cultivated throughout a lifetime if it is to stay vital and life-giving. Similarly, while aggression and love may be kin by nature, the ability to retain consciousness of that close relation and to discern and undertake faithful being-with on the basis of it is a lifetime project.

Aggression and Theologies of Power

As we have seen, in some contrast to our contemporary focus on sin and violence, biblical narrative makes clear that faithfulness to God requires and results in lives that are incredibly vital, powerful, resistive, and sometimes revolutionary. From the opening pages of the biblical record, where earth-creatures are given "dominion" and soon rebel against the limits placed upon their lives, the proper use—not forfeiture—of power is established as a topic of enormous magnitude for religious reflection. It is interesting to note that Genesis 1:26, which concerns humanity being made in the image of God, is normally invoked to urge human beings to love as God loves. Recall the verse, however, and note that power is its focus: "Let us make humankind in our image, according to our likeness; and let them have dominion." After declaring that humankind shall be made in the image of God, the text presses directly on to "dominion." The trials of discerning how to use the power of dominion not for violence but for life have been our historical plague.

Douglas John Hall provides a starting place for this discernment in his development of the meaning of *dominion*. Writing for Christians, Hall situates his argument in relation to Jesus' way of exercising power.

> We are confronted by a "transvaluation of values." The "lordship" of the Crucified, if seriously grasped, radically transforms our preconception of domination, exchanging for the concept of a superior form of being one of exceptional and deliberate solidarity (being-with), and for the notion of mastery a vocation to self-negating and responsible stewardship.[17]

Power, exercised ethically, is not for the purpose of setting ourselves apart as superior, but for joining with others. Following Jesus, we must not be hoarders but stewards of power: we do not have power to save but to use temporarily and seek to increase on behalf of future generations. In distinction from Hall, I do not see that Jesus' way of having dominion was *self*-negating. It is more accurate to say that Jesus did not use his power to protect himself from the negation others sought to impose on his views, his influence, and, ultimately, his life. Quite the opposite: he allowed power to flow into him and make of him a steady and pointed witness to the things of God. He used his power to be a courageous advocate for a radical "transvaluation of values," and negation by others was the result.

In the exercise of the power of aggression, many of us are found wanting if measured according to the picture the Gospels paint of the ways Jesus exercised power. Too often, self-righteousness characterizes our aggressiveness: we reserve our aggressiveness for those moments when we feel ourselves "a superior form of being." Few of us are practiced enough in the expression or reception of aggressiveness for it to be experienced as being-with, though, as we observed in chapter 2, aggressiveness often arises out of the desire to make substantive contact with another person. Or, the intent of our aggressiveness is solidarity, but we end up communicating self-righteousness and criticism of others more than joining in a compassionate representation of unmet needs. No, marshaling the power of human aggressiveness to the purposes of solidarity is not easy.

Thus, if a theology of power is to be adequate, the worthy kind of power captured in Hall's reframing of "dominion" must be supplemented with an unflinching examination of power's profound ambiguity and of the ways that human beings use power for doing harm. Our particular interest in this enormous area of study centers on the search for theological perspectives that help us wrestle with the three forms of the ambiguous power of aggression we have identified—violence, passivity, and vitality.[18]

Violence

We begin our theological reflection on our capacity to use our power for distortion with acknowledgment of the capacity each of us has for physical violence: obvious forms, such as abuse and murder, and also those that masquerade as roughhousing or teasing but are thinly veiled and mean-spirited physical mistreatment. German liberation theologians Dorothee Soelle and Fulbert Steffensky are among the few who speak this truth not abstractly but plainly. In a commentary on the story of Cain, the murderer of his younger brother Abel, rather than rushing to underline our responsibility to be different from Cain, they first emphasize our kinship with him.

> The Bible holds no illusions over the fact that human beings kill each other. . . . We all have a little of Cain in us. The story is not told so that we can simply say: People are just mean! . . . If we want to be honest about this story, then we would have to come to the conclusion: That's something even I could have done! That's something I have wanted to do: to really do someone in![19]

We begin here because admission—much less frank discussion—of the very common human experience of impulses to do physical harm to another is rare. The prevalence of physical and sexual violence and the damage done by it have begun to receive attention, not only in society at large but also in religious circles. However, I would argue that, in general, we fail to personalize these issues adequately, perhaps especially in religious communities. We regularly push into unconsciousness our own violent impulses and behaviors. We typically respond with reflexive denial when someone we know is accused of violent behavior. We deftly ascribe physical violence to more distant others, especially the "sick" or "criminal." There is a shocking level of naiveté among Christians about the incapacity of our religious beliefs to contain our violence. This is true in spite of the historical fact that Christians have not only been as violent as any people, especially in the arena of ethnic and religious violence, but also have commonly used "Christian" beliefs as a rationale for that violence.

Of course, in addition to physical violence, we use power violently in more hidden, indirect, and even subtle forms, such as psychospiritual maltreatment and abuse. However, from a theological point of view, emotional violence is no less sinful than more dramatic forms of physical violence, since it damages the human spirit. Psychospiritual forms of violent power are arguably more prevalent than physical forms of violence, yet, on the whole, as a society we are less aware and equipped to intervene with emotional violence than with physical violence. Two examples—one interpersonal and one systemic—must suffice. Interpersonal emotional abuse, which includes neglect, is often the precursor of sexual abuse and physical forms of domestic violence.[20] But emotional abuse has received less attention and is less well defined and understood than physical violence.[21] An excessively literal interpretation of the sixth commandment—you shall not murder (Deut. 5:17)—likely has contributed to our greater legal and ethical tolerance for emotional abuse than physical abuse. Social systems, Soelle notes, institutionalize our violence on a daily basis and carry it out indirectly. Soelle emphasizes the difficulty of retaining consciousness and concern regarding this phenomenon, but even if aware, individuals typically feel helpless to effect change.

> In the modern context, sin has in general more the character of passive, unwilling letting-it-happen, not having done anything about it, rather than a deliberate action. Our killing and stealing is in most cases unconscious and unwilling. We hardly notice that we are killing and stealing. But we are unconsciously woven into an economic context which presupposes thieves and murderers if it is to function.[22]

Reasons for our misuse of power in violence are complex. But I suggest that one of the most significant factors relevant to this work is that we use physical and emotional violence to ward off the threat that ambiguity's uncertainty poses to our reality, perhaps seemingly, to our very lives.[23] The mere existence of someone portraying some reality other than the one with which we have come to feel comfortable and identified can evoke an impulse to destroy that person. Soelle and Steffensky put it bluntly: "Envy and hatred toward those who are different from us are behind the feeling that we all have had from time to time: I could kill that person!"[24]

Theological reflection on the potential for physical and emotional violence inherent in power is a crucial warning as we consider aggression. Religious commitments do not save us from our capacity to do physical and psychospiritual harm to another. Indeed, as we shall discuss in chapter 5, spirituality, honestly practiced, is likely to expose us all the more profoundly to the hates that plague human life. Because of the potential for destructive aggression in each of us, we must take seriously our own potential for murderousness and for inflicting physical and emotional abuse. While we must reaffirm that there is no scientific evidence for an instinct to violence, Marjorie Suchocki rightly notes the relationship between our inherent aggressiveness and the extent of human violence.

> With regard to violence, we are by nature an aggressive species, with a history of physical and psychic violence. . . . The capacity for violence is built into our species through aggressive instincts related to survival. When that violence is unnecessary and avoidable, it is sin.[25]

Passivity

An adequate theology of power also reminds us that the distortion of power about which we must be concerned is not only violence. The other "side" of power's distortion is being underpowered, neglecting to cultivate our power and/or failing to seek spiritual liberation from the efforts of others to disempower us. The most extreme form of this distortion in aggression is arguably when human beings have become bystanders to genocide. This distortion of power has at least two origins. First, conditions of oppression and violence seek to disempower those on the underside of social and personal power dynamics, resulting in an actual loss of power. The diminishment of our power in such situations is usually unavoidable to some degree. Further, however, we sometimes default on our power unnecessarily. I am not referring to situations where we relinquish our power for life-affirming purposes, such as safety (for ourselves and/or others) and mutual sharing of power in relationship. I am thinking here of utter passivity in response to human denigration (of ourselves and/or others), where our passivity has no value (does not affirm life in any way) and is thus a failure to honor the *imago dei* in humanity. Even in situations of oppression and violence, we must be cautious not to compound the disempowerment foisted on us by abdicating what power we have remaining. From a Christian perspective, we are never powerless, never without the power of the sacredness invested in us at our creation for sustenance and resistance. I develop this suggestion later.

For now, I want to emphasize that when we fail to mobilize the power we have, then we, and those around us, pay a steep price for our abdication. Soelle describes the avoidance of power as "death by bread alone," a state of apathy: "everything becomes shadowy, unimportant; it no longer tastes good; you can take it or you can leave it."[26] Carter Heyward describes the avoidance of power as "the unwillingness to bear passion" and "to suffer an active sense of power in relation."[27] Both these authors say that a dominant feature of the avoidance of power—what could also be called unethical passivity—is the unwillingness to suffer, which is not only an unwillingness to feel one's own pain but also an unwillingness to bear others up.[28] We seek to live by the lowest common denominator, quietly, in a narrow, constricted way, seeking to avoid errors and missteps. In order to achieve the avoidance of power, we must practice emotional suppression and to some degree avoid relationship: the unwillingness to bear passion is not only to have "not touched our strength"[29] but also to be, with others, untouched and untouching. Out of touch, "we break the human bond and subvert God's power in the world."[30] The ultimate result is more and more death.[31]

Why are we willing to settle for bread alone, for bleak, passionless existence? Some of us deal with oppression and our fear of ambiguity, not with violence or otherwise hoarding power but by denying or ceding the power we do have to be effectual. In this way, we may exacerbate the actual diminishment of our power. Why do we do this? Again, the reasons are more complex than we can fully explore. But one issue seems especially important for our consideration of aggression. The failure to mobilize our power often betrays a fear of power itself, especially of its capacity to effect good. While this may seem ironic, what Heyward calls our "fearful hesitation to claim our power to create" is understandable. As Heyward observes, "we have only to look around us and see the cost of creative relation—such as in the story of Jesus—to be intimidated by the realization of what may happen to us if we choose to take seriously our power in relation."[32] "Passionate people get clobbered," Heyward says. "Like Jesus."[33]

We must reckon with the reality that loss of aggressiveness, whether due to suppression by circumstances beyond our control or by way of our own sacrifice, contributes to conditions of sin and despair. External conditions that diminish our aggressiveness result in the real loss of the internal capacities and the external resources needed for fighting the conditions of oppression and violence. For example, if malnourishment results from poverty, there might be a real physical weakness that would diminish our positive aggressiveness, or the depressiveness of oppression can dull positive aggressiveness and make us compliant in unjust circumstances. This is one of the desired results of oppression and violence, I contend, that it repress the aggression of the subjugated, and not primarily its negative effects but, more important, its positive potentialities.

But perhaps more difficult to deal with is the theological mandate implied: not to sacrifice one's constructive aggressiveness, even in situations of oppression and violence. The complete repression, or sacrifice, of aggression contributes to "death by bread alone." Tragically, we contribute to and exacerbate the actual conditions of oppression and violence when we voluntarily deal with our aggression by repressing it. Nonaggressiveness is no more faithful a response than is the use of aggression to do violence. Indeed, we do a kind of violence indirectly. We do harm through failure to rally constructive aggressiveness: we stand by and do not defend ourselves or others from attack, or we fail to evoke from ourselves or others the sacred fullness of each person in which the life force of aggressiveness plays a part. Our passivity is not simply a psychological issue, not only evidence of a lack of personal self-esteem or pathological introversion. Rather, it is a loss of relationality—a failure to feel deeply, suffer with, and reach out to others—and is therefore a poignant failure to connect with God.

Vitality

Adequate theologies of power concern themselves not only with the misuse of power but also with how power can be expressed constructively. We have been considering that aggression might yield powerful vitality, and in theological discussions of vitality, we find clues for how aggressive vitality can be shaped into an influential, moral, relational force.

For theologian Edward Farley, vitality is a transformation of the passion of subjectivity, which he describes as an elemental "passion for life and meaning on behalf of the self."[34] The passion of subjectivity is not free in its essence. It is bound in a solipsistic relationship with its world. It is egocentric, captive to its own purposes and continuation. The passion of subjectivity involves interest in people and things beyond itself, but only insofar as they assist the agent in acquiring the means of its survival. If, however, one has the salvific experience of reconciling oneself to one's fragility and vulnerability—the experience of "being-founded," Farley calls it—then a kind of courage results, and it leads to two major transformations in the passion of subjectivity.[35] On the one hand, egocentricity is breached. There is a "willingness not just to face but to become something new."[36] The agent is freed to embrace a risk that might extend the identity and boundaries of the self. Connected to this, the passion for life and meaning is extended. No longer attentive to the world of others and objects only for their value to the self, the agent develops a fascination for life itself. And this is vitality, Farley says. It is hunger for life "in the midst of things," a longing to encounter the ambiguity of life as it is.[37] Not yearning only, vitality is active: it is "resistance to death, to dullness, to meaninglessness on behalf of something larger than the self."[38]

Vitality is discussed theologically under a remarkable variety of other rubrics. In the pastoral care and counseling literature, Howard Clinebell speaks of "*the growth élan,*" the basic motivation and source of energy for all potentializing,"[39] and the willingness to risk that growth "opens the door to greater intimacy."[40] Rita Nakashima Brock images powerful human vitality as "*heart.*" Heart is the "center of all vital functions, . . . the seat of the self, of energy, of loving, of compassion, of conscience, of tenderness, and of courage. . . . "[41] John Macmurray developed the centrality of *agency* to the human person and the *unity of action* to human relationship: "Now if the world is a continuum of action, and there are in it a number of agents; and if action is the determination of the future, the condition for action is a unity of intentions, and the actions of the different agents must be unified in one action."[42] Starhawk adds to the familiar trilogy of power-over, power-under, and power-with a fourth power: "*power-from-within*" "sustains our lives."

> Power-from-within is akin to the sense of mastery we develop as young children with each new unfolding ability: the exhilaration of standing erect, of walking, of speaking the magic words that convey our needs and thoughts.
>
> But power-from-within is akin to something deeper. It arises from our sense of connection, our bonding with other human beings, and with the environment.[43]

The notion of *passion* is well developed in feminist theology as a way to talk about the vitality in human power. Heyward characterizes "passion" as "power in relation": "a person of passion endures both the power and ecstasy of relation and the pain and trauma of broken relation whenever she witnesses, or is involved in, the destruction of human relation."[44] Power in relation is revealed through erotic power, which is the authority and connectedness engendered in mutual sensuality, learning to "trust our senses, our capacities to touch, taste, smell, hear, see, and thereby know . . . what is real and what is false, for us in relation to one another and to the earth and cosmos."[45]

This marvelous variety in vitality makes clear several points about aggression. Because it is a vitalizing force in the psyche-soma, it is potentially a source for the ethical use of power that faithfulness requires. However, its potential value must be cultivated. Through prayerful attention to our aggressiveness, we shape its development and employment in positive directions and relational forms, such as those just described. With this care-filled monitoring, aggressiveness can be what it promises, the origin of constructive energies for life and faith.[46]

Aggression and Theologies of Liberation

The Bible conveys in many images that faithful human beings are expected to embody life-affirming powerfulness: we are called to resist a lukewarm state, not simply to have life but have it abundantly, to take our lights out from under bushels and put them on stands for all to see. This powerfulness is not for pleasure alone. We are called to use that power to contest violence and work toward the transformation of conditions that give rise to it. In short, we are called to live joyfully, boldly, and, because of violence, resistively.

In theological discussions of liberation, we find two topics that are especially helpful for understanding theological issues related to aggression. We will begin with an exploration of resistance, where aggressiveness is subtext, and then move to a discussion of nonviolence theory, where aggressiveness finally comes out in the open in theological context.

Resistance

Resistance of oppression and the building of just, compassionate community are imperatives for those who would call themselves Christian (Luke 4:18–19).[47] Yet such a statement immediately confronts us with a paradox. Christian history and theology are plagued with "the atrocity of Christian complicity" with oppression.[48] That we have participated in various ways in hatred and injustice, however, must not be allowed to serve as a barrier to our work to transform our own practice and to our participation in the repair of the world—people, ecology, values—that we have helped damage. It does, however, make the responsibility of resistance all the more difficult. We cannot fight only the evil outside ourselves; we must rigorously identify the evil within and, in a sense, resist ourselves. What is resistance, and what might be the positive and negative roles of aggression in it?

First, resistance is a culture, not an individual way of being. Patricia Hill

Collins describes how "cultures of resistance" are built and sustained in African American community through a diverse plurality of group life: for example, through family, women's community, blues clubs, African American solidarity, and storytelling about ancestors who resisted.[49] Second, resistance requires the formation of cultures within which it can be encouraged and strategized, because oppression resists resistance.[50] We need others to help us sustain resistance in the face of the "resistance of resistance." As Collins observes, a system of domination "corrupts and distorts those sources of power within the culture of the oppressed which provide energy for change."[51] A third general point is that cultures of resistance are not "pure." They have "contradictory elements"[52] and develop in "contradictory locations."[53] Their mores typically cultivate both opposition to and conformity with injustice; the contexts in which they are nurtured are typically both binding and radicalizing. Similarly, resistance is made at least somewhat "fragile," Sharon Welch points out, by an inherent tension between skepticism and commitment: a "dialectic" between the doubt born of experiences of oppression, on one side, and the possibility born of experiences of liberative community, on the other, characterizes resistance.[54]

These points lead to some observations about aggression and resistance. First, if we expect our aggressiveness to be useful to us in resistance, we need to allow it to be tempered and directed by cultures of resistance, by the accumulated wisdom of the communities within which we stand. This is in significant contrast to the headstrong and individualistic way in which many of us go about expressing our aggression. Second, Hill's observations about oppressors' corruption and distortion of energy for change suggest that aggressiveness might be one of the tools of resistance that oppressors seek to resist. When oppressing, we may seek to distort the aggressiveness of people who protest; when oppressed, we may find aggression beyond our reach or misinterpreted, no matter how constructively we seek to express it. Finally, the fragility of resistance suggests that ability and competence in positive aggressiveness will likely come and go, and be compromised by our contexts. We do well to expect this dialectic and make our times of nonresistance times during which we cultivate the strength and courage to rally energetic initiative again in the struggle for liberation.

James Newton Poling's identification of three categories of resistance—silence, language, and action—provides a framework for considering different forms of constructive aggressive resistance.[55] How can silence resist oppression? Silence on the part of the oppressed, frequently and erroneously interpreted as indifference or acquiescence, "often . . . points to the presence of threats of spiritual and/or physical violence."[56] Thus, silence can be the refusal to put oneself in harm's way and thus the resistance of oppression's violences. But resisting through silence can also be proactive. Silence can be reflective, space to think, space in which to cultivate the liberated consciousness that can provide internally a "sphere of freedom" where self-definition can be crafted, in contrast to the many spheres of oppression, where others' controlling images are imposed.[57] In this sense, silence truly is a "way of knowing" and one not less than or preliminary to, but foundational and sustaining of, other ways of knowing.[58] Using silence to resist oppression can be distinguished from common conceptions of "passive aggressiveness," where silence is typically used to manipulate others or avoid responsibility.

Common conceptions of aggression rarely include silence. Aggression is stereotyped as spilling over into blustery speech and action. Those who are silent are often assumed to be—and told they are—not aggressive enough. The role of silence in resistance suggests that such an interpretation of one's aggressiveness or aggressive potential may be wrong. Aggressiveness can be expressed as an internal rigor of thought and consciousness, and silence in the aggressive state can represent wise caution and self-protection. Those who say no words have not necessarily lost their voice or their aggressiveness.

In a second form—language—resistance begins to multiply into myriad forms according to individual proclivity and community tradition. "Talking back,"[59] "honest speech" (telling secrets and speaking the truth),[60] retelling stories of resistance ("dangerous memories"[61]) and thus keeping them alive, daring to disagree with oppressors, writing books and preaching sermons that "enable and sustain people to *be* good news in the larger world"[62]—all these are forms of resistant "speech." The power of language for resistance rests in several dimensions. Language is the power of naming—and thus the capacity to exercise some control over—the shameful truth about oppression that unjust systems would prefer go unspoken. Language is resistant when we use it to articulate the ambiguity of our lives and thus refuse "the seductions of segmenting life, reducing life's complexities to false simplicity, or collapsing life's paradoxes to immobilizing moralisms."[63] Through the language of resistance, the crafting of liberated consciousness continues through dialogue that confirms or sharpens one's perceptions about oppression.

Aggressive speech can be an effective medium for the language of resistance. Without aggression, we may be unable to utter resistant speech. The challenges of "speaking the truth to power," of naming one's own perceptions of injustice, are known to most of us. Without the initiative and boldness that aggression imparts, we may be unable to speak and thus miss an opportunity, however small, to interrupt the cycle of violence. But that is, indeed, part of the challenge of resistant speech: how to speak the truth without unnecessary violence. Aggressive language is only constructive, this discussion of resistance reminds us, when it does not play into or further oppression. If we allow our aggressiveness to explode in order to have the nerve to speak or are unprepared to receive the aggressiveness of others where appropriate, resistant speech may disintegrate into verbal violence that does not liberate. Yet we must also acknowledge that, even at its most constructive, aggressive resistant speech is usually difficult for listeners to receive, especially without becoming defensive.

Cultivating a relationship to one's own aggressiveness is one of the best preparations for "hearing into speech" the constructive but still pain-filled and
protesting language of resistance—whether our own or others'.

When resistance takes the third and final form, we shall consider—action—
first and foremost, the actions of resistance must be committed to survival, and
not just for oneself but for one's community.[64] The will to survive is a form of
resistance but, paradoxically, often requires the appearance of compliance. But
that which looks like compliance by the oppressed is often a mask that shields
from view a second kind of resistive action: the fostering of communities of
solidarity, safe spaces, where liberative living is being experienced and is giving birth to the capacity for more resistance.[65] Resistive action is most directly
transformative of evil when there are resisters who attempt to engage oppressors in relationships of accountability instead of treating them with abuse and
alienation and thus continuing the cycle of violence that breeds oppressors.
Such resistance engages in movement toward evil and justice, in order to
counter the movements against and away from right relationships that are endemic to injustice. Resistance, says practical theologian and homiletician Christine Smith, "is not an act of standing still and defending ourselves against the
evil that surrounds us, but . . . a movement into it, and through it."[66]

Three aspects of this discussion intersect meaningfully with our thinking
about aggression. Aggression, which we have identified as our will to survive
and thrive as persons and communities, can be one of the deepest sources of
resistant actions committed to survival. Further, that which looks like a sacrifice of aggressiveness and the "too much compliance" about which Winnicott
was so concerned may, on closer look, be a form of resistance (the aggressiveness of survival or camouflage) and ought to be supported, not "healed."[67]
Also, Smith's words evoke the most basic aspect of aggression, our capacity for
movement and for engagement. Aggressiveness is one of the major dimensions
of our humanness that, if nurtured into a secure self-knowing and a source of
strength and courage, can empower us to find some small way to contribute
to the reparation of the world. We can marshal our muscles and build a house
for the homeless, gather our energies and offer to help care for people with
AIDS a few hours a week. This is aggressiveness at its least provocative and
yet most positively resistant—pitching in, lending a hand. We are "God's arms
and legs," doing concrete acts of love and justice in the world.[68]

Nonviolence

Within the theological discussion of liberation, the most explicit and extensive references to aggression's values are found in nonviolence theory, where
aggressiveness is named as one of the qualities that imparts to nonviolent
resistance its power. Martin Luther King, Jr., described the effective resister as
physically nonviolent but "dynamically aggressive spiritually."[69] King called for
this aggressiveness on the basis of his interpretation of the teachings of Mo-

handas Gandhi's philosophy of *satyagraha* and *ahimsa*. *Satyagraha* means, literally, "clinging to truth." Truth is soul or spirit, the "only correct and fully significant name for God."[70] Holding steadfastly to truth inevitably brings one into contact with evil. In nonviolence theory, then, *satyagraha* is more specifically the resistance of evil through soul-force. Forms of aggressiveness are an essential part of this soul-force, as we shall discuss in a moment.

Living as a *Satyagrahi* is an achievement of maturity, as is the positive and love-infused expression of aggression. But also like the aggression that is part of it, *satyagraha* "is an attribute of the spirit within. It is latent in every one of us."[71] Gandhi was insistent that *satyagraha* is a way of life children can practice and should be taught. Like Winnicott, he emphasized that children must experience early the energies of efficacy that lie within: "It will not be denied, that a child, before it begins to write its alphabet and to gain worldly knowledge, should know what the soul is, what truth is, what love is, *what powers are latent in the soul*."[72] *Ahimsa* is love, the "most durable power"[73] and the "regulating ideal" of nonviolent resistance.[74] Just as aggression and love must be fused to achieve an honorable vitality, without love it is not possible to seek or find truth.

In nonviolence theory, resistance is not passive and is not simply the absence of violence. Liberation is achieved through active resistance. "We cannot be content with reactive nonviolence," New Testament scholar Walter Wink says, "it must be proactive, aggressive, militant."[75] When King calls for dynamically aggressive spirituality in resistance, he recalls four central tenets of nonviolence theory that can be elaborated as spiritual guidance for cultivating the dynamic and nonviolent aggressivity that powered the civil rights movement.[76]

First, nonviolence does resist. The need for aggression's energy, boldness, and creativity comes through in the many qualities identified by Gandhi and King as essential for effective nonviolent resistance: unswerving devotion to truth, industry, active mind and emotion, concentration, discipline, physical fitness and strength, consistency in opposition to evil in every sphere of life, courage, insistence, noncooperation, humility, and patience. Physical violence is always avoided by those committed to the dynamically aggressive spirit of nonviolence. But if physical forms of aggression are unavoidable, the person committed to nonviolence strives to make them detentive and not destructive. We may have to use our aggressiveness to detain someone from doing violence, but it is never moral to seek to do someone harm in the process.[77]

This daunting repertoire of capacities makes clear that before spiritually aggressive nonviolence changes the opponents, it has already wrought a change in the aggressiveness of those who seek to practice it.[78] One should not aggressively resist if one does not also have the aggressiveness to bear the consequences of resistance. But the relationship between dynamically aggressive spirituality and the spiritual maturity to take responsibility for one's aggressiveness is circular. Cultivating internally a dynamically aggressive spirit builds up a sense of what King called "sombodiness"—self-esteem and self-respect, previously unsuspected potency and bravery, and dignity.[79] "Sombodiness" makes one's aggressiveness mature, even distinguished, as was seen in the dignity of the civil rights movement. Ironically, being aggressive in mature, dignified, nonviolent ways will likely make us seem maladjusted. As King forewarns: "You will be called an impractical idealist or a dangerous radical."[80] But King also tells us that the dynamically aggressive spirit of nonviolence so manifests the "most durable power" that we should pray to be maladjusted to evil in ways like this.[81]

Second, aggressiveness should be found not in attack of the opponent but in "toughmindedness"[82] toward the evil deeds they are doing. Nonviolent resisters do not aggressively attack people or their ideas. They do, however, aggressively attack problems. In nonviolent resistance, transformation is effected by appeal to opponents' reason and conscience by one's willingness to sacrifice nonviolently for what one considers truth. Constructively aggressive nonviolent resistors do not coerce others. Neither does King's counsel to focus on "convincing" others get to the heart of the constructive power of a dynamically aggressive spirit. Constructive aggressive resistance is often convincing, but that is a byproduct more than its essence. Rather, constructively aggressive nonviolent resistors focus their aggressive energies to bring forth in themselves an authentic vitality that seeks to reflect the power and the compassion of God. Nonviolent aggressiveness is constructive and convincing only if it conveys something of the mysterious ambiguity and relationality of God.

Though we are often inclined to fault others when our aggressive appeals fail, nonviolence theory turns our attention back to ourselves. "Lack of capacity to convince the opponent shows defect in oneself."[83] If our constructive aggressiveness is not effective, it is rarely constructive simply to pile on more of the same approach or "turn up the heat." If our aggressiveness is not effective, then we are best advised to cultivate more of the qualities mentioned previously—somebodiness, patience, humility, physical fitness, discipline, and so on—so that our aggression becomes less alienating and more irresistible.

The third and fourth points are closely aligned. Take account of your opponent's welfare. Avoid not only physical violence but also "internal violence of spirit"[84]: be civil, courteous, and gentle in resisting. These principles are arguably the most difficult of all, in part because they require such skill in aggressiveness. It takes a great deal of precision in aggressiveness to be tenderhearted toward one's opponents, even as one is diligently seeking to represent one's own feeling-thoughts with vigor. It takes a very creative aggressiveness not to humiliate one's opponents or retaliate in a struggle to win, but to keep one's destructive aggressiveness focused on the forces of evil.

As demanding as these spiritual disciplines of nonviolent but resistive aggression are, nonviolence theory maintains they can be learned. One foundation is the cultivation of the assurance that truth, the God one pursues, is found not only in one's own means of resistance but also in the ways of others. When one's own approaches are not working, one can use aggressiveness relationally, reaching out for the help of another, rather than using aggression to "turn up the heat." Another spiritual resource for the cultivation of nonviolent aggression is preparation for loss. To be a *Satyagrahi* means transformation of ourselves and thus giving up "the former things." Without preparation for letting go of these old ways, violence is likely to creep into our aggressiveness as we grasp for ways to hold on, subvert loss, and evade grief.

Biblical scholar Walter Wink agrees that the source of this dynamically aggressive spirituality is an essential part of "engaging the powers" and offers an additional strategy. Wink says that "creative aggression" is found not in the repression of our aggression but in closing the inner gap between "anemia" and violence. He suggests that a source of creative aggression is in the practice of disciplined, prayerful reflection on our impulses to violence, with the aim of owning their powerful energies and transforming ourselves from being either passive and indecisive or full of arrogance and fury, to being proactive and resolute.

> For years nonviolence has been falsely caricatured as anemic, chicken-hearted, and passionless. . . . We need to be able to bring anger, power, passion, and an iron intransigence to our nonviolence. Our inner violence, transformed, becomes an indispensable aggressiveness, a sense of strength, that prevents us from blowing our stacks out of a sense of powerlessness or impotence. . . . When we fully know from within that we will not back down, we no longer have to bluster and fume.[85]

Aggression and Theological Ethics

> When I was young and bold and strong,
> Oh, right was right, and wrong was wrong!
> My plume on high, my flag unfurled,
> I rode away to right the world.
> "Come out, you dogs, and fight!" said I,
> And wept there was but once to die.
>
> But I am old; and good and bad
> Are woven in a crazy plaid. . . .[86]

As the veteran in Dorothy Parker's poem suggests, human battles, public and private, are frequently predicated upon the belief that right and wrong can and must be differentiated: truth is this and not that; evil is there and not here; I am right and you are wrong; I am bad and you are good. Note also the initial individualism and isolation of the veteran and others referred to as "dogs."

Then again, a lack of healthy aggressiveness, including but not limited to the inability to fight necessary battles, may suggest that a person or community has become immobilized in the face of ambiguity's overwhelming possibilities, including the demands of relationship. If violent aggression is the attempt to fight against and defeat ambiguity, lack of healthy aggressiveness can be seen as having surrendered to and been defeated by ambiguity. Aging, reflective veterans of all kinds of battles—military conflicts, divorce, corporate takeovers, theological combat—not infrequently report that experience in living teaches them that life is more ambiguous than they thought in their youth. "Good and bad are woven in a crazy plaid."

The ambiguity and relationality of aggression raise a crucial theological problem and opportunity: how can we live out the image of God's powerfulness without distorting it, either through violence or through passivity and a lack of vitality? Ultimately, there is no generally applicable rule to save us the painstaking work of discerning the meaning and value of aggression in each circumstance. I have been working with the following guideline: in my view, we use our aggression negatively when we direct our energies and powers toward nonessential and/or unconscious violence;[87] we use our aggression positively when we direct our energies and powers toward affirming and defending life in both its personal and collective dimensions. Beyond this general principle, we can sketch a few points that lead in the direction of an ethic of aggression. I must present these points one at a time, but each is made important and tempered by the others.

First, like power, aggression just is. We do not have a choice whether we shall be aggressive. Theologically, aggression is a given aspect of our createdness, and refusal to deal with the complexities of aggression is refusal to deal with the complexities of the holy. This most basic aspect of an ethic of aggression requires that we develop a deep consciousness of the complex nature of aggression in us, in others, and in relationship and then act out of that consciousness. Misuse of aggression here is to fail to develop such awareness and action.

Second, aggression's is-ness is profoundly multivalent and ambiguous. It can help and harm and is usually not simply good or bad but has all at once positive and negative effects, so it is wise to have mixed feelings about aggression. Misuse of aggression here is to refuse to wrestle with its multivalency, to refuse to see, for example, the woundedness of the violent and the cost of victory. In ethical behavior, we acknowledge aggression's ambiguity and take responsibility for it. This means we have crucial choices of conscience about how we express and respond to aggression and must seek always to understand the context in which it is experienced. Primarily, this means seeking always to mend the splits in aggression, the split between violence and vitality and, especially, trying to (re-)braid love and aggression where it has become split in consciousness or action. This bridging of the opposites is the surest way to build a base from which we can choose the most moderate and tempered expression of aggression effective in the situation at hand. But it is arguably the most difficult challenge posed by aggressiveness. Under the conditions of complexity and taboo that surround aggression, it is, as Winnicott claims, a psychospiritual achievement and a sign of maturity to hold onto consciousness of and responsiveness to the essential relationship between love and aggression and to develop the ability to reweave these aspects of the psyche that social and existential forces tear apart. Spiritually, it is a profound challenge to trust the mystery and numinousness of aggression. It is an even greater challenge, I think, to trust that human beings can show one another grace when aggression's ambiguity leaves us hanging somewhere between right and wrong.

Third, aggression generates and reflects relationality. Perhaps a derivation from the Golden Rule is more to the point: be aggressive unto others as you would have them be aggressive unto you. The most general implication that arises from aggression's relationality is that mutuality is one of the most crucial goals of an ethic of aggression. One of the most destructive and immoral employments of aggression is to cut off the possibility of another's constructive aggressive expression. Conversely, one of aggression's most transformative moments is when it empowers us to make room for, nurture, and protect each other's constructive aggressive expression. As African theologian Mercy Amba Oduyoye puts it, "make the other strong and you will be strong, we shall all be strong together."[88] Many specific points could be made here, but let me touch on just two that seem often to be overlooked. First, because of aggression's relationality, ethics requires that we analyze how social arrangements of power construct different meanings and values of aggression in different situations. Second, aggression often is conceptualized as pushing others away, and this often is its effect. But aggression's relationality begs us to consider how an aggressive expression—ours or others'—might also be an attempt toward meaningful, honest engagement.

Fourth, aggression is power and, because of its ambiguity and relationality, can manifest in a range of powerful expressions from violence to vitality. Aggression testifies to our having been endowed at our creation with power—physical, emotional, and spiritual life, movement, and effectuality. Here the misuse of aggression is the denial of our power—it is unethical to shirk our powerfulness, to refuse to acknowledge either the constructive engagement or the harm made possible through our aggressiveness. However limited by genetics, traumatic relationship, or oppressive environments, we are never completely powerless: God never leaves us. Ethics requires our refusal to fully sacrifice or fully indulge our aggressiveness. Ethical behavior is engagement in an ongoing search to identify and embody the vitality invested in us and to identify and braid love into the means by which we do harm through excesses or insufficiencies in aggressiveness.

Surely the most obvious unethical use of aggression is in the destruction of life and well-being. If aggression is, as Winnicott suggests, an expression of the

life force, then our aggression expresses its truest purpose when it helps au-
thor and defend life, a fifth crucial element in an ethic of aggression. Because
of aggression's relationality, this authorship and defense must not be individualistic or ideological but can be ethical only when it honors life wherever it is
found, as widely as possible. This leads to a guideline: when encountering aggression, ours or others', it is helpful to try to discern whether some real or perceived threat to life has led to the aggressiveness. Further, an ethical
employment of aggression requires that we consider how aggression can help
build among us a vital sense of aliveness, the development of strong selfhood
or a strong system, a healthy sense of power, and the capacity to get and stay
connected to others with integrity and honesty. Spiritually, having access to the
constructive aspects of one's aggression is a tremendous resource for spirited,
soulful living and for imaging sacred power with a minimum of distortion.

Finally, ethical engagement with aggression requires us to acknowledge
that, however constructive, aggressive expression is enormously demanding.
Reckoning with aggression is hard work, and its difficulties typically push us
to the edge of our maturity and capacity to be faithful. Unethical behavior here
is to fail to make emotional and relational preparations for these difficulties, to
expect others to smoothly agree to all our resolutions in aggression, or to accuse others of a lack of love when they show the strains of the hardships that
inhere existentially to aggression. To conduct ourselves ethically in regard to
this aspect of aggressiveness is to offer ourselves and others the humble patience, understanding, and good humor that binds us together in the face of
existential difficulties. To the degree that we can begin honoring ambiguity instead of only resisting it and to the degree that we can rely upon relationality
for connection instead of scapegoating, then even the demands of aggression
will deepen the bonds of love.

The next chapter provides opportunity to practice intellectually some of
these principles of an ethic of aggression. Because we cannot understand aggression fully except in relation to its cultural context, in chapter 4 we analyze
aggression in the cultures of gender and race.

4

Aggression in Cultural Context: Gender, Race, Oppression

Snips and snails and puppy dog tails:
That's what little boys are made of.
Sugar and spice and everything nice:
That's what little girls are made of.
—Anonymous

In Europe, the black man is the symbol of evil. . . . The torturer is the black man, Satan is black, one talks of shadows, when one is dirty one is black. . . . [A]nd on the other side, the bright look of innocence, the white dove of peace, magical heavenly light. A magnificent blond child—how much peace there is in that phrase.
—Franz Fanon,
Black Skin, White Masks

In our way of dealing with the internalization and disposal of aggression there is a largely unconscious, one-sided splitting off of certain emotional mechanisms. The dynamics of this are largely socially determined.
—Margarete Mitscherlich,
The Peaceable Sex

"SANDRA," A EURO-AMERICAN, feminist woman, raised as a Christian, has been plagued for years by fears of being attacked when alone. She fears rape, darkness, and, for reasons that are at first inexplicable to her, the rage of people of color. When she dares image her attackers, they are black.

Feeling shame, despair, and confusion, she tries to find some understanding and resolution with her pastoral counselor. Their sessions explore her upbringing as an upper-class, white girl reared in a community racked by racial, sexual, and economic discrimination. She feels so much guilt about racism that perhaps, she ponders, her imagination produces scenarios of the attacks she fears she deserves because of her complicity in racial injustice. Yet, as a female raised in a culture where violence against women is epidemic, she also fears being the victim of male violence. She feels mostly defenseless against the possibility of other people's violence. She also fears the eruption of her own rage: she was taught that nice Christian women do not get angry, and so her rage threatens both her self-image and public persona. She is sure her rage will at least alienate others and probably injure them. Recently, weary of the hold her fears of vulnerability and violence have on her, she is deliberately, courageously putting herself in situations where she must wrestle with her terrors. Still, she says, "I feel like such a chicken."

Sandra's story reveals how difficult it can be to reckon with aggression in our cultural contexts because aggression is costumed in the mores and prejudices of the multilayered societies in which we live. Themes of aggression can be identified in several dimensions of her struggle: in her exhaustive and exhausting vigilance because of the reality of male violent aggressiveness toward women; in her self-punishing guilt about the real violence of white supremacy; in the pressure she is under to conform to the sexist stereotype of the nice girl; in her fear of acknowledging her rage; in her difficulty rallying enough constructive aggressiveness so that she does not feel "like a chicken"; and in her gutsy determination to confront and take on her terrors.

Thus far we have been examining aggression in mostly general terms. In this chapter, I explore what it means to reckon with aggression's ambiguity and relationality in cultural context. My argument is in three parts: (1) socialization shapes aggression in children in ways that help create and perpetuate systems of oppression, (2) dominant cultures use distorted aggression to enforce oppression, and (3) subordinated cultures (and recovering dominants) use aggression to resist oppression.

Like Sandra, most of us find that multiple identities cause us to count ourselves among both the oppressed and the oppressors. We experience aggression in complex layers: we are violated by aggression, we use aggression to violate others, our passivity threatens loss of aggressiveness and submission, and our aggressiveness surges in resistance to oppression. In this chapter, I discuss three of these interlocking levels of aggression's functions in the systems of domination and subjugation that we experience: aggression is used to create and perpetuate oppression, to enforce oppression, and to resist oppression. Taken together, these three levels comprise a "politics of aggression"; aggression is not simply a psychological category or personal issue: the common good, and lack thereof, is at stake.

The specificities of harm-causing aggression have been fairly extensively re-searched in terms of cultures of ethnicity and nationality.[1] Therefore, I take a different tack. I examine the socially constructed cultures of race and gender—and the attendant phenomena of white supremacy and male domination—in or-der to identify some of the positive and negative functions of aggression in the dynamics of domination and subjugation.[2] If we look at the differences gender and race make in aggression, the meaning and politics of aggression come into sharper relief. In order to be as detailed as possible in our discussion of white supremacy and racism, I have chosen to focus on the relationship between Euro-Americans and African and other black Americans in the United States, though some of these observations may well shed light on other situations of white domination. Because my goal is to create a discussion that addresses systemic as well as individual manifestations of white oppressiveness, I use the con-struction "white supremacy and racism." When I speak of *white supremacy,* I am referring to the social and historical system of white privilege and white racial oppression, not specific hate groups characterized as White Suprema-cists—arguably the "identified patients" of the sick system of white racism.

A few general observations begin our discussion. First, much research has been conducted on the difference sex and gender socialization make in child-hood aggression, in contrast to the meager amount of research on whether race or racism makes any difference in childhood aggression. (As follows from the argument of this book, I do not consider the plentiful research on violence among children of color to be an adequate basis for discussion of how the cul-tural socialization of children's aggression might play a role in racial oppres-sion.) Thus, in the first section, where we examine the role of aggression in creating oppression through the socialization of children, we focus on social-ization through gender and sex-role stereotyping and use our findings to sug-gest a few implications for race and white supremacy. In the second section, where we examine the role of aggression in enforcing oppression, I focus on white supremacy and racism, partly to lend balance to our discussion but pri-marily because I contend that the role of male aggression in enforcing sexism is far better understood and more widely recognized than is the role of white aggressiveness in enforcing white supremacy and racism.

Second we will be able to think of individuals and groups that are exceptions to the general trends I identify here, especially those in the first two sections. They are reminders that the forces of socialization exist but are not always suc-cessful in securing complete compliance. I believe it is crucial both to seek to identify general trends in socialization and to hold fast to the awareness that what we observe about trends is not true of all individuals or groups. We can hold fast to the witness of such exceptions as one means of relativizing the power of so-cial dynamics and trends and the claims of research regarding them. We consider later in the chapter the ways these trends and stereotypes are resisted.

Third, I have chosen to jump into the process of socialization of aggression at the point of childhood because it is the closest we can get to the beginnings of aggression's cultural meanings. Further, it is an opportunity to consider further the enormously important question of what we teach our children about aggression. Socialization certainly continues into adulthood. It is my contention, however, that, for those who do not learn dominant cultures' rules of aggression in childhood, socialization is augmented with threat and punishment in adulthood. Thus, we consider the socialization of aggression in adulthood when we turn to the use of distorted aggression to enforce systems of domination and subjugation. We further consider socialization in adulthood when we look at patterns of aggressiveness in the resistance of oppression.

Aggression and the Creation of Oppression: Gender Socialization as Example

Through socialization, cultures impart meanings to aggression and communicate norms for aggressive behavior. More exactly, examination of the cultures of gender and race reveals that socialization shapes children's aggression into stereotyped patterns of behavior that help create—and perpetuate through the life span—behaviors of domination and subjugation. As noted above, we focus in this section on the effects on human aggression of gender socialization and sex-role stereotyping because there has been little investigation into the racialization of aggression during children's socialization. I close this discussion with some hypotheses regarding the implications of these dynamics for white supremacy and racism and for the socialization by African American parents of their children's aggressiveness.

The description of the socialization of aggression in girls and boys that follows relies on the work of British psychologist Anne Campbell.[3] After many years of studying delinquent girls, Campbell developed an interest in the everyday aggression of "typical" women and in the reasons why aggression is so different in women and in men. Her analysis is based heavily on tape-recorded conversations that took place in groups of women and groups of men who knew each other. She asked them to talk about their experiences of anger and aggression. Campbell does not identify the ethnicity of her interviewees or in any substantial way analyze the difference race makes to her findings. We will append some reflections about this difference to her argument. The minimal information we have about race and the socialization of aggression suggests that, while African American children are affected by some of the gender dynamics Campbell identifies, other factors Campbell does not address are operating as well, and we turn to those later in the chapter.

Campbell's main thesis is that aggression is so different in women and men because, in general, aggression has different meanings for them:

> For women aggression is the *failure* of self-control, while for men it is

the *imposing* of control over others. Women's aggression emerges from their inability to check the disruptive and frightening force of their own anger. For men, it is a legitimate means of assuming authority over the disruptive and frightening forces in the world around them.[4]

Similarly, for many women, aggression threatens humiliation of the self and loss of relationship, while for many men aggression represents enhanced esteem, valuable autonomy, and increased control over those with whom the man is in relationship.[5] Women and men learn these different meanings in childhood, grow to shape the private and public world according to them, and, to the degree they have contact with children, teach these meanings to the next generation. As we will see, girls tend to learn that aggression is "expressive"— it signals emotional upset or lets off steam—while boys tend to learn that aggression is "instrumental"—it is a means to an end, a way to get something the boy wants, especially from another person.[6] How do these lessons get taught, and why do children accept them? To answer this question, we look at trends in socialization, focusing on gender dynamics in the interactions between typical parents and their children. But it must be remembered that wherever children go—day-care centers, church school classrooms, playgrounds, toy stores, libraries, television sets, their picture books—they encounter women and men (and their products) ready to teach them similar lessons in aggression.

At birth, male and female babies are not noticeably different in their aggressive expression: as one measure, females babies "cry and scream just as much" as male babies.[7] In their first years of life, since most young children are still cared for primarily by women, both boys and girls learn from those women approximately the same lesson: aggression is the result of the inability to tolerate frustration; while it is understandable, the child must learn self-control. Women typically teach children that the expression of aggression is an undesirable loss of self-control and an expression of meanness to other children. Control of aggression facilitates continuity of relationship, while its expression threatens isolation.

Campbell argues that two factors begin to cause differences in aggression in children, both having to do with gender identity development. One factor is that parents consciously and unconsciously begin to shape their children's behavior to reflect sex-typed characteristics. Research indicates that, though this will later change, mothers of infants are relatively heedless of sexual difference when it comes to disciplining their young children's negative aggressiveness.[8] But there is evidence that fathers are more disturbed than mothers by cross-sex behavior, especially in their sons.

Campbell cites a study in which researchers brought young children into a playroom stocked with sex-typed and, I would add, aggression-typed, toys. "Boy-toys" suggested stereotypically aggressive activity: figurines of soldiers and war vehicles, cars and a highway, a cowboy outfit. "Girl-toys" included a doll house, toy stove and cooking accoutrements, and dresses and hats for playacting, suggesting nurturing activities not usually thought of as aggressive. Parents were brought into the room to watch their children play, and researchers observed parental reactions. Fathers were likely to show disapproval of cross-sex play five times more often with boys than with girls. Mothers showed no sex difference in their level of disapproval.[9] This paternal behavior has been observed with children as young as twelve months.[10] There is evidence that fathers especially are shaping their young sons away from behavior that is characterized as nonaggressive and feminine, and toward behavior that is negatively aggressive and characterized as masculine. It is interesting to note that evidence suggests that fathers might not be discouraging aggressive, masculine behavior in their daughters, at least at this early age.

A second early factor in the development of differences in aggression is the child's own discovery of sex difference and the contrasting tasks in gender identity development that boys and girls typically face. Sometimes even before the age of two, children are already aware that sex makes a very important difference.[11] A study by psychologist Beverly Fagot and colleagues has demonstrated that the single factor of gender identity makes a difference in the aggressiveness shown by children, especially girls: while boys' recognition of their gender identity appeared to increase their aggressiveness slightly, girls' recognition of their gender identity decreased their aggressiveness significantly.[12] Campbell interprets this to mean that gender identity translates for girls to "*suppression* of their own aggression."[13] However, the picture she paints of why gender identity has this significant impact suggests that the suppression of girl's aggressiveness is not accomplished simply through the girl's free choice.

What are the different pathways followed by boys and girls in the socialization of their aggressiveness? If he is typical—if his primary caregivers are female—the discovery of sex difference sends a boy into a period of searching for an understanding of what it means to be male and not female. To the extent that his father or other caring males are not physically or emotionally available to him—and sadly, this is the case for many boys at the age of two or younger—the boy may first learn by means of the negative, what he is not. He "learns by counterimitation to avoid and eventually to disparage qualities" associated with being female.[14] As noted in the study cited previously, if close male influence exists in his life, it is likely only to continue this avoidance learning. Maleness is taught by discouraging femininity: "Don't be such a girl!" This is understood to mean that the boy is teetering on the edge of the not-male: impotent, unaggressive, and insubstantial. Even young boys enforce within their peer groups this avoidance learning: much more frequently than girls, boys reward their playmates with approval for gender-appropriate behavior and react with derision to sex-inappropriate play: "That's dumb, boys don't play with dolls."[15] Avoidance learning is critically important in the perpetuation of sex-role stereotyped behavior.

It hinges on the evocation of anxiety and even fear. . . . It is a form of learning that is deeply emotional and powerful. Because it successfully deters the individual from ever attempting to breach the taboo, it guarantees that he will never discover that it is safe to do so.[16]

But the boy also seeks to construct a model of masculinity from the maleness he sees around him. He learns from the men he knows and the cultural images of maleness—television, toys, books, and the like. And these tend to surround him with the rationalization and veneration of male aggression in forms that are typically violent. Even when fathers seek to give their sons other models, they cannot shield their boys from the overriding cultural message that violently aggressive images are images of masculinity. "It is men, not women, who slay dragons and fight in defense of the innocent."[17] Furthermore, reinforcing that the relational world of his mother is taboo and poses a threat to his masculinity, the boy is deluged with images in which "emotion and masculinity are cut off from each other in the images of the men he sees."[18] Finally, from these images he learns a lesson about aggression that his mother typically is not teaching him—or his sister. Aggression is an exhilarating experience of action, potency, power, and control. Moreover, aggression gets results.

Once he learns these lessons, his mother's ability to exercise "relational control" over his aggressive misbehavior begins to diminish.[19] Because of aggression's worth, both in itself and for propping up his fledgling gender identity, he begins to value it more than he fears "the dire consequences of aggression as described by his mother—the rupturing of relationships, the loss of another's love, the possibility of injury inflicted on a friend."[20] Instead, from cultural and personal messages about masculinity, he learns that "instrumental control" is what matters, which requires not that he *sacrifice* his aggression but that he *follow the rules* of aggression. He will be taught by culture "whom he can fight, what constitutes an adequate provocation, how to conduct his violence, and when he can reasonably expect condemnation, recognition, or glory for his actions."[21] Finally, his aggressive behavior gets him a lot of attention. Whether at home, school, or play, whether viewed with affection or judged as a liability, a boy's aggressiveness attracts the attention of adults. And since to openly court the affection or relationship of others is feminine, a threat to masculinity, many boys seek relationship in the only masculine way they feel safe to seek it—through attention-getting aggressive behavior that is often risky or destructive.

What happens with girls? If she is typical—if her primary caregivers are female—a girl's search for the meaning of gender identity does not initially require a differentiation of herself from mother and femaleness. Instead, the girl typically seeks to become more like her mother and other females she observes. If her mother is reasonably available and their relationship is even moderately affectionate, further attachment typically characterizes the first step in her gender identity. Though determining her distinctiveness from her mother will be a later challenge, even that task is likely to be accomplished more through "relationship-differentiation" than through separation.[22]

This means that she learns her lessons about aggression in the context of relationship, through the "linking of learning and loving."[23] But it must be said that she does not learn a great deal more from her mother about aggression. After the early learning that mothers typically seek to instill in their children—that aggression must be controlled, that it risks harm to others and relationship—girls' learning in aggression is essentially over.

> [A girl] remains selectively tuned in to a female wavelength, searching for clues to femininity and to aggression. But she finds little to examine. After her mother's early censuring of overt displays of aggression, there is a gaping void. The most remarkable thing about the socialization of aggression in girls is its absence. Girls do not learn the right way to express aggression; they simply learn not to express it.[24]

Other aspects of culture reinforce the message that a girl's expression of aggression is not significant. Girls are much less likely to criticize each other for cross-sex play; there is not much concern about girls who are tomboys,[25] at least as long as it is believed to be a passing phase. Teachers do not criticize and restrain girls' aggression as much as they do boys'.[26] Like the boys, most girls also notice that in cultural productions it is normally males and not females who "slay dragons and fight in defense of the innocent."[27] When aggressive women are portrayed in the media, their greatest interest value lies in their being oddities. They are often shown failing to be aggressive as successfully as men and thus becoming objects of ridicule, and finally, in need of rescue by men. These examples point to what Campbell suggests is the most direct and basic cause for girls' decrease in aggressiveness: "It is ineffective at the most basic level—that of communication. When girls aggress, nobody notices and nobody reacts. . . . So the little girl learns not only that aggression is emotionally dangerous but that it doesn't get her what she wants."[28]

In adulthood, these early patterns blossom into distinct gender differences in aggression. Women find it hard to claim healthy assertion; men find it hard to admit the costs of their forcefulness. Women are more likely to direct their aggressiveness toward members of the opposite sex, men toward those of the same sex. For men, the display of aggression is a public event, while women avoid public displays and tend to be aggressive in private. Women worry about the morality of aggression itself, while men worry about the morality of the rules: "Did I fight fair?" For men, aggression presents the possibility of winning or losing, but women tend to feel they have lost by being aggressive at all.[29] These different ways of being aggressive force "a behavioral wedge" between women and men.[30] The sexes speak different languages in aggression, and so the ways of one sex are inexplicable to the other, resulting in distance and danger.[31] Finally, psychologist Carol Gilligan notes that gender differences in aggression may reveal different evaluations of a dangerous relationship.

If aggression is conceived as a response to the perception of danger, . . . men and women may perceive danger in different social situations and construe danger in different ways—men seeing danger more often in close personal affiliation than in achievement and construing danger to arise from intimacy, women perceiving danger in impersonal achievement situations and construing danger to result from competitive success.[32]

In part through these early lessons in aggression and their implications for adult behavior, basic tenets of sexism are laid down. As Campbell puts it,

In society at large, men's and women's ways of handling provocation put this same conflict on a grand scale.

More is at stake here than a simple sex difference in perspective . . . . As long as men hold positions of power it is *their* beliefs that count.[33]

Campbell's observations here need to be supplemented. Yes, it can be argued that men's beliefs about the meanings of aggression for males and for females "count" more in social structures of power than women's. Psychospiritually and relationally, however, both women's and men's beliefs and practices regarding aggressive behavior result in a complex mixture of value and loss. What are some of these specific results?

Control is required of a man to prove his masculinity, the concept of a woman's femininity barely exists if she is not acquiescent. Men's aggression is made a vulgar centerpiece of culture and callously commodified, women's aggression is marginalized and blithely derided, mischaracterized, and denied.[34] Denuded of much of their aggressiveness, many women are made needlessly vulnerable, and men—at least in wartime—are forced to provide self-sacrificing protection.

Males are socialized in aggression from their earliest years to spend their bodies for attack and to devalue their own lives just enough that they will be able to make this physical sacrifice, if it is needed. Women's self-sacrifice is expected to be spiritual more than physical; females are socialized in nonaggressiveness from their earliest years to spend their emotions to keep the peace and to devalue their own souls so much that they are ready to make this daily sacrifice. Rarely are men or boys explicitly taught the skills of relational connection. Rarely are women or girls explicitly taught the skills or relational boundary-setting. Real men must know instinctively how to fight; real women must not want to learn to fight. Men who show too much relational connection and women who seek out training in fighting (for example, through martial arts or the military) are typically seen as potentially suspicious exceptions. Despite the general trend not to teach girls and women the skills of psychospiritual aggressiveness or physical self-defense, it is not uncommon that women are expected to be able to fight off men who attack them. Tragically, women who are raped or otherwise attacked frequently are racked by guilt for not having the aggressiveness to fight off their attacker; women's aggressiveness is more likely to flood them with emotionally violent and erroneous self-blame than with the assertively self-respecting anger that would be appropriate. Men are reluctant to see the domination in their aggression; women are reluctant to protest aggressively. If women do protest too aggressively, men have skills in aggression that serve to threaten or retaliate. If unchanged, current patterns of socialization in aggression can and will hold these gendered distortions of aggression in place.

Some aspects of this discussion have only limited applicability to African American families and their socialization of children's aggressiveness. For example, for the most part, neither male nor female African American children see positive images of African American aggression in the media. Much of what they see is extreme, either passivity and acquiescence or anger and violence directed against the self or other members of the black community. Additionally, lack of access to social power and the reality of racist violence require many African American mothers and fathers to teach their children much more finely tuned lessons in aggressiveness than are required for white children.

An example of the ambiguous complexity of this issue for African American parents, worth reading in its entirety, is lesbian feminist Audre Lorde's reflections on the challenges of raising her daughter and, especially, her son, amid many-layered oppressions. "Raising Black children—female and male—in the mouth of a racist, sexist, suicidal dragon is perilous and chancy. If they cannot love and resist at the same time, they will probably not survive."[35] The aggressiveness she must teach her children—resistance—must be braided with love and with ability both to define themselves and to "let go." Thus, she teaches her son the very things Campbell says socialization in aggression seeks to deny to boys—the capacity to articulate his feelings, the valuation of women, and the ability to choose not to fight and to feel good about it. To do this, when her son is scared by bullies, she shares with him a story from her own childhood through which she tells him about her own feelings of impotence and fear, to his relief and disbelief.

> It is as hard for our children to believe that we are not omnipotent as it is for us to know it, as parents. But that knowledge is necessary as the first step in the reassessment of power as something other than might, age, privilege, or the lack of fear. It is an important step for a boy, whose societal destruction begins when he is forced to believe that he can only be strong if he doesn't feel, or if he wins.[36]

Lorde challenges the picture Campbell paints. She exemplifies a mother teaching her son something other than an instrumental interpretation of his aggression and other forms of power. She also challenges the notion that the only other alternative is an expressive interpretation. Lorde seeks to teach her son to be "who he wishes to be for himself" and "to move to that voice from within himself, rather than to those raucous, persuasive, or threatening voices from outside, pressuring him to be what the world wants him to be."[37]

But, of course, neither do African Americans fully escape the pressure of socialization that distorts aggressiveness. Psychiatrist Charles A. Pinderhughes's description of how whites conditioned blacks during slavery also captures the aggressiveness of white racist socialization of blacks' aggression. Pinderhughes's analysis is so pointed and poignant that it is worth quoting at length.

> By rigid use of punishments and rewards of an especially convincing nature, blacks were conditioned to accommodate to whites, to trust whites, to distrust themselves, to have affiliative bonds to outsiders (whites), and to have [negative] aggression, criticism, and derogation directed toward themselves. They were required to employ a value system which undermined and destroyed self-esteem. They were programmed toward a poor fit with institutions in the broader culture except in servile roles and often toward a poor fit with the needs of their families. They were conditioned toward sacrifice rather than mastery, toward defeat rather than toward success, toward accommodation rather than initiative, and usually toward incompetence rather than competence. This culture and social structure were defined and imposed by white outsiders who systematically prevented the development of internal power to control, protect, and meet needs while needed resources were withheld or used in disorganizing ways.[38]

Especially with adults, socialization to systems of domination and oppression is often accomplished through violent means, as Pinderhughes's reference to "punishments and rewards of an especially convincing nature" genteelly suggests. Continuing our examination of aggression in cultural contexts, the use of violent aggressiveness in the enforcement of oppressive conditions within cultures is the focus of the next section.

Aggression and the Enforcement of Oppression: White Supremacy and Racism as Example

Once the socialization of aggression in children has helped to put the dynamics of domination and subjugation in place, aggression is also used by dominant classes as a tool of enforcement. It has long been accepted that aggression plays a part in the dynamics of prejudice.[39] But in discussion of domination and subjugation, aggression is too often identified with only the most direct, physical, and violent of encounters. Therefore, the full spectrum of aggression's violence normally is not identified. Further, concentration on aggression's violence fails to identify the role of other distortions of aggression in systems of domination and subjugation, especially passivity. Because domination and subjugation are systematized in culture, many people participate in its violence by doing nothing to counter it.

My intent is to show how a range of aggression's distortions—from overt violence to lack of responsiveness—plays a role in the enforcement of systems of domination and subjugation. Though my focus on the scope of aggression's violence necessitates only brief attention to any particular form, I believe that there is heuristic value in having the wide spectrum of aggression's distortions in domination and subjugation arrayed before us. Increased ability to identify the full range of distorted aggression in systems of domination and subjugation will enable us to better understand the most subtle forms of oppression and why many marginalized people say that conditions are improving, perhaps, but not substantially. I first discuss five forms of violent aggressiveness: physical, economic, religious, emotional, and internalized oppression. I then turn to the violence of passive aggressiveness and examine it under three rubrics: inaction, avoidance of conflict, and guilt.

In this section, I concentrate largely on the distorted aggressiveness in white supremacy and racism, though similar dynamics can and have been shown in sexism. I try to communicate in this discussion that the aggressiveness exercised in white supremacy and racism (as in other systems of domination) is distorted but not rare, sickening and not limited to actions of those identified as sick. As Alexander Thomas and Samuel Sillen, authors of *Racism and Psychiatry,* point out, "all kinds of people can be and are racists: normal and abnormal, paranoid and nonparanoid, aggressive and passive, domineering and submissive."[40] Only by seeing that white supremacy and other systems of domination are kept functioning by the everyday actions of average people will we have a chance of comprehending the damage done by these systems and finding our way toward just relations with one another.

Violent Aggressiveness
in White Supremacy and Racism

We begin with what womanist ethicist Emilie Townes calls "the spectre of the noose."[41] Violent physical aggressiveness, real and threatened, is one of the oldest tools in the enforcement of white supremacy and racism. As we observed in chapter 3, human beings are inclined to deny or minimize the potential and reality of our involvement in murderousness. And, indeed, how difficult it is for white Americans to grasp the potency of hundreds of years of epidemic white-on-black physical violence. For generations, kidnappings, beatings, rapes, and lynchings, and the threat of these, were tools used to hold blacks captive physically and psychologically. White-on-black hate crimes continue this enforcement still. Additionally, though not named as such, the physically aggressive enforcement of white supremacy continues when African Americans are without warrant physically accosted or beaten by law enforcement officials. But as Townes's image suggests, the historical reality of physical violence against blacks is psychologically efficacious even four centuries later; that is, in order to enforce white supremacy, average white Americans in the twentieth century do not need to be as physically violent against blacks as were their ancestors, because the fact of whites' capacity to be physically violent against blacks has been well established by our ancestors' violence against blacks. Like toxicity seeping into the water supply from drums of poison buried generations ago, the threat of violent physical aggression may never be completely removed from the environment of African American and Euro-American relations. The current generation will pay for the creation of a toxically racist environment and its clean-up—even if another racist act was never committed.

Because many white people have access to the structures of social power, they engage in violent aggressiveness far more often in what are, for the dominant class, experience-distant forms. There is, for example, economic violence. White aggressiveness in the marketplace greedily eats up more than a fair share of profit. Statistics from the 1993 U.S. census bear this out dramatically. The median net worth of whites was $45,740, of blacks, $4,418. Disparity exists even among the wealthiest citizens. Within the richest fifth of U.S. citizens, white citizens have a median net worth of $123,350, black citizens, $45,023.[42] Economic aggressiveness is normally considered only a sign of ambition and hard work, though it may be just as much a sign of insatiability and self-service. The economic greed of the dominant class also contributes to disproportionate poverty among women and people of color. African-American women suffer economic violence doubly, and consequently they are the poorest of the poor in the United States; "almost half of all female-led African-American households live in poverty."[43] These economic disparities translate into violent consequences for African Americans and other people of color. For example, less adequate health care causes blacks, on average, to die younger than whites.[44] And the toxic waste to which I referred earlier is not metaphorical only: the location of toxic waste dumps and the chronic and fatal health problems they cause show a pattern of environmental racism that maims and kills.[45] The violence done through callously aggressive economic and other structural forms of racism are experienced by many African Americans as "contemporary lynchings."[46]

Another form of violent aggressiveness is religious in nature, where the violence can be understood as destruction of the well-being of the soul. We could cite many examples here, but I will focus on the violence done through portraying divinity in the image of the dominant culture. Clinical psychologist Na'im Akbar identifies a range of psychospiritual meanings and costs of portraying God as white.[47] For whites, imaging God as Caucasian threatens a confusion of white physical characteristics with the nature of God and can lead to "ego inflation."[48] In this normally unconscious state, persons have an inflated sense of their own rights and value and a decreased ability to exercise critical judgment in regard to their own actions or the actions of people with whom they are identified. Akbar claims that portraying God in their own image has had just this effect on whites: "It began to destroy the person's natural humility."[49]

"Once the person gets an inflated idea of who he is and what he is, then he does not have the capacity to naturally correct himself."[50] Whites demonstrate this inability to be critical and self-corrective especially, I would add, in matters relating to race and racism. White ego inflation contributes to many other forms of destructiveness as well: imperialistic evangelism and parasitic colonization, for example.[51] We see here several aspects of aggressiveness: arrogance, entitlement, and, ultimately, self-destruction.[52]

Caucasian images of God can serve to keep in place this sense of inflation among whites. Moreover, imaging God as a controlling Caucasian can undermine white's perception of African Americans' agency, effectuality, and ability to act with constructive aggressiveness in forms such as self-determination, control of community resources, independent thinking, or leadership.[53] Finally, Akbar argues that the persuasiveness and intransigence of Caucasian images of God threaten African Americans with a form of "psychological slavery" if accepted: "Once you begin to believe the divinity is somebody other than you, then you are put into a psychologically dependent state that renders you incapable of breaking loose until you break the hold of that image."[54]

All the types of violent aggressiveness we have touched upon have emotional ramifications, of course. But in closing this brief discussion of violent aggressiveness in white supremacy and racism, I want to discuss three forms of emotional violence specifically. First, we must give weight to the "microaggressions" committed by whites, offenses that are so quick or subtle that they may happen outside the consciousness of both whites and African Americans but nonetheless are disrespectful, exploitative, and thus violent.[55] Microaggressions happen commonly, for example, in the marketplace: when sales associates wait on white customers before serving black customers, when security guards suspect black customers before suspecting whites, and when management renovates stores in predominantly white neighborhoods before renovating stores in predominantly black neighborhoods. The dailiness and subtlety of these indignities are reason for African Americans to be constantly on guard. In this way, their consciousness can be held captive with the threat of racial oppression.[56] Thus, so-called microaggressions are an especially effective form of control: they are micro in form, compared to gross forms of racism, yet they are macro in effect.

Second, a great deal of the emotional violence of oppression can be attributed to whites' inability to bear consciousness of or take responsibility for the ways that they and their ancestors have used their aggressiveness to do violence. Instead, there can be seen widespread defensiveness and, more technically, the use of defense mechanisms to deflect this awareness. Whites' psychological *defense* of self often constitute *offense* for African Americans. It must suffice to enumerate just a few of these defense mechanisms, describe their function in dealing with aggressiveness, and provide examples of their role in the enforcement of white supremacy.

In *projection,* people unconsciously attribute to another person or group the aggressive feelings, thoughts, and impulses they personally feel and deem unacceptable, thus alleviating their sense of responsibility for that aggressiveness and protecting the ego. Whites project their violent aggressiveness and thereby seek to absolve themselves of responsibility for it when they project onto African Americans their own fury and then pathologize the personhood of African Americans by consistently portraying them as enraged. In the defense mechanism of *intellectualization,* people seek to rise above disturbing aggressive feelings by avoiding their emotional power and talking about them in complex conceptual categories. In the context of white supremacy and racism, intellectualization is accomplished when whites persist in talking about racial violence in abstract categories and refuse to engage in feeling-filled conversation about the real suffering racism causes African Americans and whites. Intellectualization is violent by violating feelings. In *reversal,* people defend against their own violent aggressiveness by behaving as if the actual situation is inverted. Reversal is a defense mechanism much in vogue in white supremacy in recent years: to deflect attention from their own impulses toward racial exclusion, it is not uncommon to hear whites accuse African Americans who support affirmative action of "reverse discrimination." In *repression,* people seek to put their violent aggressiveness out of consciousness. In the context of racism, whites' repression leads to denial of African Americans' experience of the painful reality of white supremacy and racism. In *displacement,* people defend themselves against violently aggressive feelings or impulses by displacing their emotions or actions onto a less threatening target. For example, whites filled with impulses to do physical harm to African Americans but finding that prospect too threatening, have displaced their violent aggressiveness onto the burnings of crosses, churches, and other property.

A third form of emotional violence in white supremacy and racism—and one of the most guileful—is directed at resistance movements. Not infrequently, dominant classes suppress the protest of subjugated classes with physical, economic, or religious violence. The more frequent and often shrewder strategy of oppression is carried out through emotionally destructive tactics: ignoring, mocking, minimizing, and mischaracterizing protest movements. This strategy is shrewder because it is slower and more subtle than other forms of oppression and undermines the roots of the protest—a healthy sense of power, esteem, and rights in the oppressed—simply by refusing to engage the protest as a form of meaningful communication. For example, white reaction to the Million Man March revealed exactly these emotionally violent tactics: within white communities, the momentum in black communities building toward the March was widely ignored, the intent of the March to offer black men the opportunity for community and confession was not infrequently mocked, the importance of the event for making change was directly questioned and thus minimized, and by mischaracterizing the March participants as mindlessly aligned with the politics of its organizers, the integrity of the participants was impugned.

Finally, perhaps the most hideous aspect of the use of violent aggressiveness in the enforcement of domination is that it sets up the oppressed to participate in their own subjugation through internalized oppression. Certainly, the majority of oppressed people resist this ruse. We will turn to the constructive aggressiveness revealed in resistance shortly. But we are exploring here this very surreptitious violent aggressiveness perpetrated by oppressors, thereby seeking to avoid one of the traps of this form of violence—being distracted from dominants' culpability in this form of violence by focusing on the "complicity" of the subjugated in their own marginalization. Thus, our goal is to understand better that violent white aggressiveness has the potential to set in motion a violent chain of events within oppressed communities and individuals. Whether or not the oppressed fall victim to it, the potential violence done by internalized oppression remains one of the weapons of violent aggressiveness in the arsenal of the dominant class.

I close this discussion of violent aggressiveness in white supremacy and racism with consideration of two forms of internalized oppression that threaten blacks in the United States: the vitality-draining effects of "psychological slavery" and the peculiar violence of identification with the aggressor. Again, though our focus will be on the manifestation of these dynamics as a result of white supremacy and racism, internalized oppression is a form of violent aggressiveness that serves to enforce oppression in most cultures of dominance-subjugation.

Introjection is the primary psychological dynamic that gives internalized oppression its power. Because the psyche has the capacity and tendency to project and introject bits of experience, the experience of being treated violently by others is not infrequently internalized, taken into the identity of the self. In chapter 2, we saw that the introjection of forms of aggressiveness encountered in others serve, among other functions, to assist individuals in constructing a strong and effectual sense of self and gaining a sense of control over negative aggressiveness experienced internally and in relationship with others. In normal and healthy circumstances, human psychospiritual formation takes place in part through "borrowing" from one another forms of aggressiveness and building oneself in relationship to "bits" of the aggressive other; this is much like the typical process scholars and artists and athletes go through—they borrow the most vital and courageous "bits" of the accomplishments of others to build up the strength and boldness in their own unique body of work. Additionally, when in a chronically traumatic situation, one poignant means the psyche provides victims to sustain some sense of protection and comfort from otherwise inescapable violent aggressiveness is to exercise power and control through taking the experience of traumatization into the self and taking over the role of the dominatingly aggressive person.

One of the most dramatic examples of violent white supremacy and racism and the enforcement of oppression through introjection can be seen in the violent effects of the legacy of slavery. Psychologist Na'im Akbar discusses these dynamics in *Chains and Images of Psychological Slavery*. As Akbar observes in his opening pages, the story of slavery contains not only agony but also the image of humanity's "greatest triumph over conditions of the flesh."[57] But the maiming violence of chattel slavery threatens an even worse form of slavery, which Akbar describes forcefully.

> The slavery that captures the mind and incarcerates the motivation, perception, aspiration, and identity in a web of anti-self images, generating a personal and collective self-destruction, is more cruel than the shackles on the wrists and ankles.[58]

Akbar argues that distortion in eight dimensions of African American life—work, property, leadership, clowning, personal inferiority, community division, family, and color consciousness—have their roots in white enslavement of blacks. The violent aggressiveness of chattel slavery distorted sacred dimensions of human life: work was distorted into punishment, property denied, leadership destroyed, creativity mockingly coerced into buffoonery, persons dehumanized, communities conquered through division, families decimated, and skin color cursed. These "chains and images" can bind African American psyches and communities in contemporary time: working may feel like slavery, unemployment like freedom; the accumulation of personal property may be pursued rather than the accumulation of more substantial forms of community power; indigenous leadership is sometimes regarded with suspicion; persons tend not to take or present themselves seriously; class divisions rend African American communities from inside; families struggle just to create basic bonds; color prejudice infects black communities. Evident in many of these dimensions is the use of violence to distort dimensions of life where healthy aggressiveness might have been fostered but was instead often derailed or kept from taking root, especially in the context of family, community, work, and leadership.

Akbar's discussion suggests that the psychological wounds inflicted by the violent aggressiveness of slavery must be tended because the failure to do so further extends slavery's power to harm. Akbar emphasizes that the strength of character and resilience shown by Africans in slavery suggest that, in addition to the wounds, African Americans have tremendous resources for breaking loose from these psychological chains.[59] Both factors suggest qualities of healthy aggressiveness. More exact identification of the elements in the strength and resilience of African Americans yield a model for healthy human aggressiveness in general, as we will soon see in our consideration of resistance.

A more specific form in which violent aggressiveness can be internalized is described by psychologist Amos Wilson in a book provocatively titled *Black-on-Black Violence: The Psychodynamics of Black Self-Annihilation in Service of White Domination*.[60] Wilson is especially interested in the psychosocial meanings of the criminality and violence carried out between blacks, especially by young black males. As part of his discussion, Wilson explores the notion of identification with the aggressor, a concept developed by psychoanalyst Anna Freud in a book in which she explored the many levels of psychological defense in situations of anxiety.[61] In this mechanism of defense, one seeks control over an anxiety-producing relationship or circumstance by assuming the violent or threatening behavior (and sometimes attributes) of the aggressor, transforming oneself "from the person threatened into the person who makes the threat."[62] In threatening another, one passes on the threatening experience by revenging oneself on a substitute.[63] It is significant to note that Freud first recognized identification with the aggressor in children's psychodynamics, that it involves a passage from passive to active, and that the anxiety felt may be in regard to a threat anticipated in the future.

When African Americans use this defense mechanism, Wilson calls this process "inculcating the beast."[64] The "beast" inculcated is, at one level, Eurocentric supremacism and racist hostility toward African Americans. But Wilson argues that it is not so much the beast (hatred of Africanness) that is desired but the power of the beast. At the heart of the identification is a desperate and furious search for the power to direct one's own life and an escape from the powerlessness and other forms of degradation imposed in white supremacy and racism.[65] The beast's violence is sometimes adopted as a model of how one secures and maintains power over one's own life in white supremacy and racism, through contempt, subjugation, and destruction of African peoples. Yet this identification is paradoxical: "While he [the young black male identified with his aggressor] imitates his White father he resents his father's power and his own subjugation to it, and at the same time holds utter contempt for his own cowardice, for he does not dare to take power from his father."[66] Where white supremacy and racism have set in motion this tragic chain of defense, other blacks become the substitutes for the rage he feels he can direct neither toward the white establishment nor directly toward himself. However, Wilson argues that through killing others and living dangerously, the black-on-black criminal courts his own death; he does so in part because he is "steeped" in white supremacist/racist guilt and has, unfortunately internalized whites' wrongdoing, and in part because of a sense of shame, secondary to the humiliation of subjugation.[67] In this way, the enforcement of oppression is extended without direct action. Violent aggressiveness is still the means, but the (largely invisible or hidden) oppressors' hands appear unsullied. The aggressiveness of the oppressed is perverted into destruction of themselves and their people.

While space allows us only to name them here, all these dimensions of oppressive violent aggressiveness can be traced in the culture of gender: the prevalence of physical violence against women, the "feminization" of poverty, and the religious tyranny of exclusively male images of God. Emotionally violent aggressiveness against women is seen, for example, in the daily microaggressions of the objectification of women in advertising, in males' defense mechanism of emotional isolation, and in the mocking or exaggeration of women's protest of sexism.[68] The internalization of oppressors' violent aggressiveness against women can be seen concretely in the prevalence of eating disorders in women and more elusively in the chronic low self-esteem and excessive guilt feelings plaguing many women.

Passivity in White Supremacy and Racism

Distorted aggressiveness is manifested in white supremacy and racism not only directly, in violent domination, but also indirectly, in passivity and lack of response. The white supremacy and racism we discuss here is sinful in the sense identified in the last chapter: a letting-it-happen attitude, not speaking up, not taking action. Joel Kovel describes two kinds of racists: "dominative" and "aversive." "The dominative racist . . . resorts to direct violence; the aversive racist . . . turns away and walls himself off."[69] Feminist theologian Susan Brooks Thistlethwaite identifies a third kind, the "recovering racist," a person who is consciously and proactively antiracist.[70] As Thistlethwaite's terminology suggests, recovering racists are always recovering[71] and are never without complicity in systems of racial domination and subjugation. This section explores the ways in which distortions in the aggressiveness of aversive and recovering racists may contribute to white supremacy and racism. We will explore three types of aggression's distortions: inaction, avoidance of conflict, and guilt.

Inaction is the failure to mobilize any aggressiveness, which leaves us unable to reach out and make contact. Without the vitality, initiative, and courage of aggressiveness, we isolate ourselves and in the process isolate the other from us, in a way that is liable to be experienced as hostile. One form in which inaction manifests in white supremacy and racism is ignorance. Many whites steadfastly refuse to inform themselves about the lives of African Americans or about the realities of white supremacist and racist violence. Another form of the subtle violence in inaction can be seen in the failure to establish contact with African Americans: ignoring them and treating them as if they are invisible, as in walking by on the street without a polite "good day" or even a nod of acknowledgment. To "recognize" others is—by definition—to show basic respect for others by acknowledging their existence, inviting them to speak, showing appreciation for them, and/or affirming their stature. Thus, though many whites fail to cultivate consciousness of this dynamic, the simple refusal to recognize the other can be experienced as a form of violation.

A second kind of passivity can be seen in avoidance of conflict. If inaction is the failure to engage African Americans and the issues of white supremacy and racism, then avoidance of conflict is disengagement from relationship begun but then found too threatening. Whites may approach relationship with African Americans but then withdraw when the issues get too hot. In this manifestation of white supremacy and racism, passivity distorts aggression in two directions: disengagement and merger.[72]

Three arenas of avoidance of conflict can be identified in white supremacy. Whites sometimes disengage from themselves, fearing and avoiding inner turmoil over white supremacy and racial conflict. The violence here is that if whites seek relationship with African Americans without doing their own inner work about racism, they will likely exploit African Americans emotionally: unable to speak their own feelings, they may expect African Americans to give them voice.[73] Second, whites sometimes avoid conflict with African Americans, fearing honest words of pain, anger, or confrontation. The violence accomplished through avoidance of conflict with African Americans might be felt as the absence of something, like the lack of authentic emotional honesty and intimacy in relationships between African Americans and whites. Finally, "recovering racists" sometimes avoid conflicts with white racists or in other ways fail to intervene in racism. The violence accomplished through this aspect of aversion is more obvious: doing nothing to stop racial violence and by silence perhaps communicating agreement.

One final aspect of aggression's distortion in aversion or being underpowered is encountered in whites' ineffective guilt about white supremacy. Feelings of guilt and shame may indicate genuine remorse for the horrors of white supremacy and real concern for the needs of others. But preoccupation with the sense of guilt can also indicate a fear of discovery and punishment or a primary concern for one's own wounded self-esteem. Here whites are attuned primarily to their own needs, and guilt and shame have become ends in themselves, a masked form of passivity.

> All too often, guilt is just another name for impotence, for defensiveness, destructive of communication; it becomes a device to protect ignorance and the continuation of things the way they are, the ultimate protection for changelessness.[74]

If whites do consider themselves genuinely complicit, then some form of reparation is the appropriate response, and one that requires a healthy relationship to aggression—one's own and others'. But in the passivity of being guilt-ridden, whites have no relationship to their actual aggressiveness, only to exaggerated estimates of its dangers and lack of consciousness about its value. In these three ways—inaction, avoidance of conflict, and preoccupation with guilt—white supremacy is enforced indirectly through the sacrifice of relationship to aggression.

Certainly it is not only in relation to white supremacy and racism that we can identify bigoted people in aversive and recovering forms. Such distortions of aggression into passivity can be identified as well in relation to, for example, gender socialization and sexism, though space allows us merely to name some illustrative situations here. Since gender segregation is minimal compared to racial segregation, women and men rarely avoid connection with one another; thus, in sexism, inaction cannot be so easily characterized as the mere failure to reach out and make contact. But passivity manifests quite commonly when men and women fail to make substantive intellectual or emotional contact with one another, ridiculing rather than inquiring into the interests of the other, or remaining silent rather than voicing any resistance when misogyny is evident and sex-role stereotypes are being enforced.

As with white supremacy and racism, avoidance of meaningful conflict runs rampant in regard to gender socialization and sexism, in the same forms we identified in white supremacy and racism: avoidance of internal conflict in regard to values associated with gender and sex, of conflict with the opposite sex, and of conflict with people engaged in sexist, misogynist behavior. Widespread utilization of a caricature of the angry woman enables us to identify another aspect of the avoidance of conflict that also functions in white supremacy and racism: blacks and women who express even modest amounts of anger over the oppression in which they live are often immediately caricatured as all at once engorged with rage and fearsome, comical and inept, and hypercritical and self-centered. This misrepresentation serves to avoid conflict in at least two ways. This general discrediting of the caricatured groups serves to undermine their credibility and authority to confront the behavior of others. Further, the constant exaggeration and ridicule by dominants of anger expressed by oppressed groups is also used in an effort to distract perpetrators and victims alike from investigating the actual circumstances of the anger and perhaps discovering warrants for its existence.

Finally, unhealthy and thus ineffective guilt is displayed paradigmatically by the batterer: in the cycle of domestic violence, the batterer's remorse typically is expressed with heartfelt drama, but it is almost always ineffective. It rarely leads to the constructive reflection and proactive reparation that result from genuine and healthy contrition. That the batterer's remorse so often and so facilely translates into the emotional attacks that are prelude to physical assault reveals the remorse to be a self-gratifying and passive form of violent aggressiveness.

Aggression in the Resistance of Oppression: Race and Gender

In the face of oppression, aggressiveness is sometimes not optional but essential. In the spirit of survival, vitality, and self-respect, aggression can help us oppose domination and repair subjugated lives. This is true whether we are, in a given context, those subjugated or those who are "recovering dominants." We utilize here the three forms of resistance discussed in chapter 3—silence, language, and action—to examine how aggression is used to resist and repair in cultures of gender and race. At the outset of this discussion it is crucial to note that, because of aggression's ambiguity, resistance is not usually easy to be around, even when it is necessary and constructive. Moreover, resistance is sometimes carried out in tragic and violent ways. Aggressive resistance merits no romanticization.

Silence in Relation to Dominants

When we examine the resistance of silence within the cultures of gender and race, a particular kind of silence comes into focus, that of oppressed people's temporary withdrawal from dialogue with people in dominant classes, for the purposes of increased engagement with other members of their own groups. Participation by women in consciousness-raising or other feminist groups and participation by African American people in black-only religious communities serve as examples of this kind of silence. The creation of these women-only and black-only communities is often interpreted by dominant classes as a negatively aggressive exclusionary tactic. But these relatively brief periods of silence in relationships to dominant classes are more often inclusionary in intent, motivated by the need of marginalized people to gain the power of feeling included in a community of people who know firsthand their experience of oppression. This is a group experience of the kind of resistive silence we identified in chapter 3, in which silence takes one briefly into safer space, where the power of oppression is lessened, and opportunity is provided to think and act one's way into new strength and pride in identity. These periods of withdrawal from relation to dominants bear resemblance to the ancient spiritual practice of "retreat": periodic and temporary withdrawal from one's everyday life for the purpose of spiritual renewal.

These periods of "silence" are often significantly interrelated with aggressiveness. First, it takes aggressiveness on the part of subjugated persons to dare to draw away for a time from nursing their relationships with dominant classes. Further, aggressiveness is at play in many dimensions of the dynamics of these groups. Nicolina A. Fedele and Elizabeth A. Harrington have identified four ways in which the connections made in women's groups can heal,[75] and we can identify issues related to aggression in all four. These groups heal by providing validation of experience, they say, and feelings often validated in women's groups include feelings of anger and rage in response to oppression. These groups also heal by empowering women to act in relationship. Power is understood here as the capacity to move and be moved in relationship;[76] as was argued in chapter 2, movement fundamentally concerns the aggressive qualities of the psyche. Women's groups help cultivate the courage and determination to act boldly and forcefully, to be aggressive enough to seek to influence others, even as we learn to contain aggressiveness so as to allow ourselves to be influenced. Further, women's groups heal through the development of self-empathy, a stance many women need to develop in regard to their aggressiveness. Finally, women's groups heal through mutuality, and in the confrontation and anger of typical group processes, women have opportunity to practice healthy give-and-take in the expression of aggression.

Sociologist Cheryl Townsend Gilkes has identified four unique practices that make African American churches "therapeutic communities," and in each of these we can also identify aggression as a subtext.[77] Black churches heal, Gilkes suggests, by offering opportunities to "articulate suffering," a part of which is communal celebration of the personal and collective strength that enables survival and resilience in persecution, and which we have identified as a kind of constructive aggressiveness. African American churches also heal by helping to "locate the persecutors," which involves a boldly aggressive naming of racist violent aggressiveness directed against African Americans and expression of the anger and rage suffered by the persecuted. African American churches heal by providing "asylum for 'acting out'": the dynamics of "getting happy" within the shelter of the church normally involve vigorous physical, verbal, and emotional expression, an aggressiveness in behavior risky for African Americans in the company of dominants but encouraged within the greater safety of black churches. Finally, like women's groups, African American churches heal by providing "validation of experience," which centrally involves the community rallying strength so that members can undertake the aggressive action of defending themselves against and protesting misrepresentation and mistreatment. Psychologist Thomas Parham emphasizes that African Americans must self-consciously "fortify" themselves and prepare for the next "storm,"[78] and in these periods of retreat from dominant culture, the aggressiveness cultivated in black religious life plays a central role in that fortification process.

Periods of silence between dominant and subjugated classes can be similarly used by recovering dominants as a time to cultivate the resources and skills of resistance. Silence provides space for members of dominant groups to reflect deeply on their attachments to the power and privilege associated with the dominance of their class and to develop the agency both to assert that power on behalf of justice and to find ways consciously to relinquish some of it to those on the margins. But the capacity to relinquish social power can happen only when we have so developed our inner strength that giving up a measure of social power does not leave us feeling weak and thus prone to violence. Access to and comfort with positive aggressiveness is an important aspect of cultivating a sense of personal agency that enables us to break our addictions to the power and privileges associated with our social rank.

Language: Rage,
Confrontation, and Conflict

Examining the cultures of gender and race for how aggression figures into resistive language immediately brings confrontation into focus. We can identify other aspects or qualities of aggressiveness in the language of resistance—assertion and directness, for example—but the rage, anger, and conflict that characterize attempts to have dialogue across the barriers of gender and race are among the most challenging forms of aggressiveness encountered in resistance and deserve our full attention here.

As we have noted, both women and African Americans have suffered from stereotyping of their aggressiveness. They have been portrayed as typically passive or, if even a moderate amount of assertiveness is shown, characterized as chronically or pathologically angry or rage-filled.[79] This negative stereotyping of aggression is a powerful tool in dominant classes' "resistance of resistance," both exaggerated anger and exaggerated passivity used to discount efforts made by women and African Americans to confront incidents of discrimination.

Thus, the first measure of aggressiveness needed by the oppressed in confrontation is the capacity to reclaim and shape one's own authentic and positive style in confrontation. By "positive," I do not mean to imply that the oppressed should or can make confrontation about oppression easy for themselves or members of dominant groups. But I am suggesting that in confrontation we encounter aggression's ambiguity and relationality; some forms of resistance are counterproductive to the just relations we seek to establish. We must be aware that negative aggressiveness in confrontation continues the cycle of violence. It is normally not only unethical but also often counterproductive and detrimental to our efforts toward liberation.

Means by which women and African Americans can shape aggressive expressions such as anger and rage into constructive tools of self-expression and confrontation have been given substantial attention.[80] One of the recurrent and less resolved themes in this literature is the necessity of dealing with rage, if confrontation is to be both possible and constructive. Isn't it enough—safer—to feel angry about injustice? Why search out our rage, that extreme intensity?

If we understand anger as rage cooled, tamed, and civilized, then anger may not have the strength to break trauma's tyrannical hold. Rage may well be the tumult that births our anger about social as well as personal trauma. In outlining the phases of suffering, Dorothee Soelle says that in order to break the hold of muteness, suffering's incapacitating first phase, we need a language of lament.[81] Rage is the most ancient dialect in the language of lament. Rage issues from a deeply rooted rebellion against suffering. Rage is resistance against numbness, an emotion of last resort to counteract the anesthetization induced by too much violence and death-dealing among us. Rage can be the fire that clears our hearts of the stubble of rationalizations that trip up our best intentions to resist wrongdoing, the emotional *via negativa* that enables us to embrace suffering and pain, out of love. Rage is a way of pushing through all the barriers that prevent us from seeing the connections between incidents of oppression: rage remembers our history of violence. Rage can get us seeing, feeling, and moving, that is, acting more alive where previously we had been acting out death. In all these ways, rage provides the self-knowledge that can make confrontation possible.

But rage is full of aggression's ambiguity. Rage can be bullish with delicate issues and emotions, when deftness and agility are also effective. Rage can be sensitive to subtle distinctions and yet does not necessarily foster the judiciousness required to discern important details and connections. Thus, rage can be advocated as root of our language of resistance but not as its vine or branch. Rage is an effective language for personal lament but rarely for constructive confrontation. Yet, knowing one's rage is foundational to the self-knowledge and self-control that makes authentic confrontation possible.

While it is normally most self-protective and strategic to reserve the expression of rage for safer, personal contexts, interpersonal and public conflicts and confrontations are a necessity in the process of resisting and repairing the damages of oppression.[82] If we desire justice, we must not simply tolerate tough, (nonviolent) aggressive exchanges but even welcome them because inner and relational friction is a nonoptional challenge on the way to repairing the damages done by oppression. Only by "excavating honesty,"[83] bearing with one another in telling the painful truths of subjugation, can we hope to lower the barriers we have made of race and gender. Though confrontation is a greater risk for the oppressed than for oppressors, confrontation does present a particular challenge to members of dominant classes. It is difficult to listen, listen hard, to the lament of rage, to truth-telling about the costs that domination by the oppressors' ancestors has wreaked on the lives of others. It is hard to "survive" this aggressiveness, to revisit Winnicott's challenge. It is hard for dominants, especially recovering ones, not to retaliate, not to be overcome with guilt, and not to demand credit for all they have done on behalf of justice. It is difficult to listen to the pain of the oppressed, especially when one or one's ancestors bear responsibility. The capacity to "hold" another's aggressiveness depends, of course, in large measure on the receivers' being not afraid of, even comfortable with, their own aggressiveness, rage-filled lament, and words of anger. This likely requires remedial work for most of us.

Action: Four Examples

Finally, aggressiveness can fuel "bold and unusual" strategies and acts that serve as constructive resistance to oppression.[84] Because aggressive actions are arguably the most familiar aspect of resistance, I simply point to four examples that portray different kinds of aggressive resistance that retain the ambiguity and relationality of aggression while remaining bold, unusual, and constructive.

The Million Man March portrays vividly the ambiguity and relationality of constructive, aggressive, resistive action. Some resistive action has its genesis in the aggressiveness of a leader, which then becomes contagious. Louis Farrakhan's vision for this march was successful in part because he was resisting the national neglect of the black man and offering him an opportunity to move, literally and metaphorically, in a strong and positive body. Few others have made such an ambitious outreach to provide uplift to black men. Because of Farrakhan's violent rhetoric against Jews, however, this resistive action was ambiguous. The march was tinged with the negative aggressiveness of Farrakhan's anti-Semitism. As noted earlier, it was also negatively tinged by aggressive white resistance to this burgeoning of black male resistance; resisting the efforts of the subjugated to liberate themselves is a form of violent aggressiveness. Still, many African American men and women who adamantly disagreed with Farrakhan's violent aggressiveness against the Jews embraced the march. Because the march was a rare opportunity to build up vitality and relatedness within the black community on a national scale, some members of the African American community labored to hold in tension, and made use of, the ambiguities of the event. Many African Americans did not downplay their differences with Farrakhan in order to support the march but rather used the publicity Farrakhan generated for "his" march to voice not only their appreciation for black men but also their disapproval of Farrakhan's attitudes and actions toward Jews. The effect of the march can be measured in the typically small but significant doses of positive relational connection injected into African American life by the march.

A quintessential example of bold and unusual resistance is found in Rosa Parks's simple and yet explosive refusal to move to the back of the bus. Where is aggressiveness in her example? Exhausted by a long day of women's work, probably feeling like there was not an ounce of aggressiveness left in her, she simply said no. Sometimes our aggressiveness is not flamboyant and vigorous but sick and tired, unwilling to take any more. One form of aggression's relationality is its capacity to inspire others, even when we are able to rally it only in modest of doses or have simply run out of energy for compliance. In a synchronicity marked with sacred mystery, sometimes it takes merely a small flicker of boldness to ignite the passion in others. As was true in the Montgomery bus boycott, sometimes the movement in aggressiveness comes not from our own bodies but from the bodies of those who are moved to gather into a wave of social protest, like the one that swelled up behind that brief encounter between one woman and one man on a Montgomery bus. Aggression's ambiguity prevents us from romanticizing resistance: this beloved story of nonviolent protest is misrepresented if we do not also tell of the lives lost, property damaged, and spirits scarred by the confrontations that ensued from Rosa Park's resistance.

A third example of constructively aggressive resistance is seen in the bold and unusual actions of women and supportive men within the women's ordination movement. Here we see aggressiveness slowly building up within individuals but even more so across whole segments of the church, uniting but also dividing persons across denominational and religious lines. Within Protestantism, the aggressiveness of the women and their advocates first took the form of advocacy within church structures. Later, it took the form of protest against church structures. Ultimately, it took the form of creating new church structures. As in the example of the civil rights movement, we are reminded that the actions of resistance typically require sustaining aggressive energies over a long period. The battle is still not over for some women and some denominations. And it is a battle; the aggressiveness that led to the ordination of women has caused fury and wounds that have not healed.

Finally, to make clear that bold and unusual actions resist even when they do not lead to national movements, I close with the example of the late Lillian Lewis, who worked as a volunteer in the Los Angeles Unified School District well into in her eighties. She rose every weekday morning at 2:30 A.M., commuted across town to the Granada Hills High School, and took up her post at the door. "Granny Lewis," as she was known to folks at the school, checked students' identification as they came on campus and then prowled the halls, keeping kids in line. She was gruff, threatened the teenagers with punishment for even small infractions of the rules, and the kids—most of them—loved her. Here the aggressiveness of an individual—her long service, her no-nonsense approach, her determined enforcement of the rules, her tough love—made a difference, day to day, in the lives of several hundred teenagers, their teachers, and their families.[85] It is a simple action any of us can undertake, to be bold enough to move into the community, unusual enough to offer our skills for free, and aggressive enough to risk new challenges.

Given aggression's many meanings and its complex effects on relationship, it makes sense to close our study with some reflections on how we can most constructively live with this enigmatic force. It is to that final task that we now turn.

5

Caring for Aggression

The remedies prescribed for the cure of aggression are always the same old ineffective repressive agents: idealism and religion.

—Fritz S. Perls,
Ego, Hunger, and Aggression

FRITZ PERLS IS RIGHT, in a way. Aggression has been widely regarded as a disease or character flaw in need of eradication. For too long the distortions in our aggressiveness have been treated with naive utopianism and theological condemnation. In such forms, idealism and religion are equally ineffective, both being efforts to get rid of or neutralize aggression. Neither increases our facility with aggression nor decreases its distortions.

But Perls is also wrong, in a way. Idealism and religion are neither essentially repressive nor completely ineffective when it comes to addressing the excesses and deficiencies of aggression. For example, unsentimental hope and an belief in the sacredness of life are powerful antidotes to the despair and cynicism often engendered in us by violence and passivity, and they impart meaning to the arduous effort to heal trauma caused by aggressiveness—and to heal aggressiveness. (Besides, Perls fails to note that we turn to idealism and religion, in part, because his own discipline of psychology also finds aggression an enigma and offers no cures.)

Is it possible to avoid both repressing aggression and cavalierly bandying it about and, instead, deal more forthrightly, faithfully, and constructively with both the violence and the vitality in human aggressiveness? In previous chapters, psychological, social science, theological, and sociocultural perspectives have provided us a multidisciplinary interpretation of the multivalent meanings and values encountered relative to aggression in experience, language, and theory. In this chapter, we consider more concretely the implications of previous chapters for human healing and growth: How do those approaches and aggression's ambiguity and relationality support, challenge, and suggest change in the ways we care for ourselves and others? How can we care for aggression in others and in ourselves?

An assumption underlying this chapter is that religious communities and individual seekers of spiritual and/or religious integrity have particular responsibilities and resources for caring for aggression. Spiritual and religious practices, along with individual and congregational ministries of pastoral care, can assist persons and groups to embody and respond to aggression in spiritually life-giving and relationally respectful ways. My intent here is to offer suggestions for tending aggression in self-care, care for others, and in the context of everyday interactions. Thus, I comment on both the cultivation of healthy aggression and on how we might care for and diminish distorted aggression in ourselves and others. Since children's aggression was given extensive treatment in chapter 2, in this chapter I focus on options open to adults who wish to gain more psychospiritual and relational maturity in relation to aggression. Because it is my priority to address a general audience more than a specifically clinical one, my reflections here, as elsewhere in the book, are written for any individual or group that needs assistance in the effort to care for aggression. While it would be valuable to explore specifically the roles of ministers, pastoral care and counseling professionals, and other clinicians in caring for aggression, I can do little more than point to or infer some implications. I do not address the clinical treatment of pathological aggressiveness, and I counsel pastoral care volunteers and professionals to seek referral and consultation when they encounter dangerous aggressiveness in those for whom they have responsibility for care (including themselves). My observations in this chapter are deliberately inferential, and I encourage clinicians to draw out appropriate implications for counseling and psychotherapy.

In order to focus our discussion, I have selected four arenas that concern caring for aggression: the healing of trauma, because trauma is widely experienced and distorts aggressiveness so seriously; maturity, because the concept of mature aggression is so unfamiliar and yet so needed; spiritual practice, because it offers such profound opportunity to encounter in relative safety the range of our emotions and values relative to aggression; and everyday conflict, because it is one of the most common and concrete arenas where the misuse of aggression runs rampant. Our goal is to identify and explore briefly some of the ways that a view of aggression as ambiguous and relational informs care in these situations and suggests change in practice. While space obviously does not permit full discussion of the role of aggression in these complex issues, I have selected these four arenas as representative of the range of reflection and action involved in caring for aggression.

Aggressiveness and Trauma

In one of their several articles on sexual abuse, Marie Fortune and James Poling make the following statement: "Abusers are persons who use aggressive and/or manipulative behaviors to enhance their position of dominance in order to coerce or control another person for the abuser's own purposes."[1] Several pages later, they make this statement: "The church must respond more aggressively to the danger facing women and children by providing victims with safety and needed resources for healing."[2] Fortune and Poling's observations about aggression in these two statements convey aggression's ambiguity and relationality and represent two critical emphases in the care of aggression in the context of trauma. We use violent aggressiveness to create or enforce traumatically oppressive conditions. At the same time, as Fortune and Poling imply, we and others often are not responding with sufficient aggressiveness to end dominating and traumatic conditions. How might we be enabled to live out such a challenging mandate, and do so aggressively but not violently? How are we to be more aggressive in this detentive way and yet not slip into the dominance, coercion, control, and self-centeredness that is abusive?

First, we must be *constant* in identifying where we and others use violent aggressiveness to create or enforce oppressive conditions: relationships that are self-serving, dominating, abusive, or traumatizing. Obviously, physical violence can be one aspect of traumatizing aggressiveness, but Fortune and Poling's reference to "manipulative" behaviors reminds us that we must not allow our naiveté and the horror of physical violence to divert our attention from the trauma of violent aggressiveness against the human spirit: economic control, religious battering, maddening microaggressions, denial, ridicule. While it is important for all of us to cultivate awareness of and take responsibility for the ways in which our aggressiveness might be dominating, violent or traumatizing, *or experienced that way,* sociocultural dynamics of subjugation make personal responsibility for dominating or violent aggressiveness especially critical wherever we are, or are perceived to be, members of a dominant group or class. Whites, males, pastors, even committees and chairpersons—power and privilege brings with it extra potential for abusing our power, being perceived as abusing power, and dealing manipulatively with the power of others. Because aggression is a form of power that is ambiguous, relational, and demanding, ethics requires us to engage in ongoing self-examination wherever we are in positions of power.

I am not saying that we are fully responsible for others' perceptions about our aggressiveness. I am saying that if another person tells us that we have caused them harm through our aggressiveness, even if it was not our intention to do so, usually the most ethical and expedient response is to seek to understand the other's experience of harm and set things right. This is both ethical and expedient because aggression is so very ambiguous and relational. Whether or not we intend consciously to harm another is important. It is not, however, all that is important in settling disputes over aggressiveness: because of aggression's ambiguity and relationality, it is just as important, from an ethical point of view, how the other perceives our aggressiveness. Furthermore, disputes regarding aggressiveness will not be resolved until all parties' experience of it has been addressed; refusal to address the perception of our aggressiveness as harmful, even if we did not intend for it to be so, is both nonrelational and self-defeating.

While we do not have total responsibility for the experience of the other, the ambiguity and relationality of aggression does make us responsible to respond to the perception of our aggressiveness. Similarly, the one who perceives violent aggressiveness has responsibility for not simply assuming intent to cause harm on the part of the other. When we are in positions where others have power over us, it is usually most ethical—where it is safe enough to do so without serious harm—to identify and name violating attitudes and actions, and to do so as the meaning of the actions to us rather than as the intention of the other. (We provide camouflage for the violence of others when we simply label them as aggressive.) If we do not have a healing and maturing relationship to aggression (our own and others'), we are likely to have little but defensiveness or passivity with which to respond to occasions that call for such truth-telling. I return to the interrelationship between aggression and maturity later.

One of the reasons aggressive people are so often perceived as traumatizing even if they do not intend to be is that most of us have wounded aggression in us. Because of patterns of socialization like the ones we have considered, few of us had sufficient experience in childhood of our aggression being survived. Since distortions in aggressiveness have been a long-standing plague in human development, few of our parents were equipped with enough healthy aggression of their own to provide primary preoccupation, survival, or necessary failures to our fledgling aggressive expressions. Consequently, few of us were adequately taught that many forms of intrapsychic and relational aggression are "survivable" and can be understood as, to some degree, necessary for life, even pleasurable. Neither have many resources existed for teaching children to discern between unnecessary violence and necessary aggression. Among other consequences, aggressiveness is split: some of us have lost access to our aggressiveness and too often become bystanders to violent aggressiveness, standing by passively, not resisting; others of us are flooded with aggressiveness and use it to belittle, attack, judge, and exclude. Thus, though more aggressive resistance of abuse is surely needed, too few of us are well-equipped to do this, whether for ourselves or on behalf of others.

Effective aggressive resistance to dominatingly aggressive behaviors will increase as we cultivate in our selves and relationships a commensurate supply of aggressive expression that is constructive-enough to set limits on violence.

And this supply of constructive-enough aggressiveness will have to be *cultivated* because, however good in the moment of creation, the capacity to use aggression for the sake of vitality and the defense of life is no longer "second nature" for most of us. Further, those of us who carry the marks of trauma where our bodies and souls have been aggressively oppressed and traumatized need special support and advocacy in the development and expression of healthy aggression, as described in more detail when we discuss maturity and aggression.

It is because of trauma that assertion is not always a strong enough response to transform suffering and wrongdoing. Where there has been trauma, especially to aggressiveness, it is nearly impossible to muster effective assertion. Moreover, however healthy and strong, assertion may not be an adequate deterrent to the traumatization of evil and violence. In both cases, the effort to heal and mature our relationship to aggression is an ethical imperative but also a grace-filled pathway to greater vitality, self-respect, and connection.

Aggression, Healing, and Maturation

Though the complexity introduced by aggression's ambiguity and relationality may be daunting, the approaches we have been considering also offer us means by which to develop our aggressiveness into more healthy and mature forms. Aggression's developmental curve, while stunted in most of us, can be revived. Out of this enormous issue of caring for aggression, I will make six observations about healing and maturing aggression that, from a pastoral theological point of view, seem to me especially promising and challenging for the healing and maturing of aggression.

We must prepare ourselves: healing and maturing our relationship to aggression is likely to seem to us a thankless task. If aggression—ethically expressed—is ambiguous, relational, powerful, life-defending, and demanding, then few people will express gratitude to us for playing a role in its more direct appearance, even if it is constructive-enough. We typically experience healthy aggressiveness in adulthood—however good for us and our world—like eating our vegetables in childhood. Efforts to heal and mature our relationship to aggression are best undertaken as a spiritual discipline: expecting that the formation will require daily diligence toward understanding the ultimately unfathomable, be arduous and uneven, be as likely to stir up relationship as to calm it, only occasionally offer an experience of joy, and make us seem odd in comparison to most others. Why do it? Like any spiritual discipline, we undertake the healing and maturation of aggression as a means, by entering into and not fleeing life's ambiguity and relationality, of drawing closer to profound mystery and thus to the sacred.

First, we have observed that childhood can be an enormously formative period in the development and maturation of aggression, but it is also true that, as adults, we can re-parent ourselves for the sake of healing and ma-turing our relationship to aggression. Where our aggression to relationship has been traumatized, self-care can repair the brokenness. Because so few of us have received adequate support in developing a healthy, mature relation-ship to aggression, we experience ourselves as excessively vulnerable or in-vincible, much weaker or stronger than we actually are. Arguably the greatest value of caring for aggression through re-parenting is that it can make us gen-uinely stronger and less likely to feel fragile and too vulnerable: from reck-oning with aggression we gain vitality and resilience, which impart to our sense of self more agency and effectuality, and thus a greater integrity of iden-tity.

What might this re-parenting and repairing look like? If the caring adults around us did not know or were not able to receive our aggressiveness and nurture it constructively, then the sacredness of our being obliges us to offer to ourselves the self-care that will heal and mature our aggressiveness. (We must also occasionally offer it to others, but I will address that matter when we consider aggression and conflict.) For example, if adults were not able to offer us primary preoccupation, then we may need consciously to choose and oc-casionally indulge ourselves in activities through which we experience tran-siently a comforting and empowering, if illusory, sense of omnipotence: for example, the exhilaration of exercising a skill, the elation of surprising loved ones with favorite treats, the gratification of lending expertise to a successful team effort. Or, if the adults around us in childhood were not able to survive sufficiently our fledgling aggressiveness, we can begin to repair our aggres-siveness by seeking to be around people who are not terrified of aggressive-ness and will support and teach us in adulthood how to discern the differences between aggressive violence and aggressive vitality. If the adults around us in childhood were too perfect or failed us too traumatically, we are likely to be too dependent or not dependent enough on the aggressiveness of others; we can heal and mature our aggressiveness through deliberately seeking out good-enough relationships, where can we experience in bearable doses the kinship of love and aggression.

A second observation about healing and maturing our relationship to ag-gression comes from our reflections in chapter 2 on the value of everyday fail-ures to the development of healthy aggressiveness. To the degree that, as they are able to tolerate it, children are gradually exposed to everyday adult failures, they are enabled to experience and build confidence in their capacity for sur-vival and necessary self-care. In adulthood, we frequently respond to every-day, nontraumatic, normal failures—of people, institutions, machines, the weather—with disdain or even outrage, as if we are not prone to such every-day failures ourselves, and perhaps indicating a lack of confidence in our ca-pacity for survival and self-care when others are less than perfect. Surprisingly, the everyday failures of others present us with opportunity for valuable expe-rience of our capacity—for brief periods—for survival, self-care, and confident aid to others, all of which require us to practice constructive aggression and thus contribute to its healing and maturation. We need our own everyday failures, and conscious ownership of them, if we are to keep a sense of humility firmly welded to our self-confidence, one of a myriad means of strengthening the kinship of love and aggression. It is strange but true to say that we need each others' everyday failures if we are not to lose, or fail to gain, access to the life-defending agency of healthy aggression.

A third observation about the healing and maturation of our relationship to aggressiveness in ourselves and others is that it will not happen if we are individualistic in our approach to aggression. That is, the harmfulness or helpfulness of aggressiveness is never adequately assessed until we have examined its effects—or absence—in contexts and cultures, and sought to respond in light of that relational and systemic analysis: for example, in interpersonal relationship, circles of friends, families, institutions, communities, or cultures of race, gender, ethnicity, religion, and class. We need to listen to the responses of others to our aggressiveness because others may perceive issues of which we are unconscious: insufficient vitality; violent or self-serving purposes. Moreover, the relationality that we have shown to be inherent to aggressive expression renders any assessments based solely on the perceptions of any one person (self or other) or context not just inadequate but also immature. Maturity in regard to aggression requires us to seek to respond nondefensively and nonoffensively to nontraumatic differences in aggression that result from relationality, culture, or other context. One of the reasons the reparenting I described above is so crucial is that it helps build up in us a strong-enough core of our own healthy aggressiveness so that we do not feel so fragile, differences are less threatening, and we are able to respond to differences in aggression with greater openness and interest. We are able to care for others' aggression as we are able to care for aggression in ourselves.

Fourth, though decisiveness and action can never wait until all ambiguity is resolved or identified, especially where violence is concerned, mature reckoning with aggression in context requires that we hold our assessments tentatively, never with a closed mind, always prepared to learn that we were not fully informed about the relational and contextual meanings and effects of aggressiveness. For example, as life in the United States is ever more pluralistic, we will encounter the lesson that different cultural contexts can render opposite interpretations of aggression. In some cultures, for example, eye contact and directness are considered healthy aggression, while in others such behaviors are considered rude or even combative; in some cultures, loud and intense speech is experienced as aliveness, in another it is experienced as evidence of trouble. When women and men, whites and blacks, or other diverse cultures encounter each other, healing and maturity in aggressiveness manifest in our ability to survive, mutually show respect for, and learn from our differences in nontraumatic aggressiveness.

A fifth observation: healing and maturation in relationship to aggression also manifest in our capacity to evaluate and take responsibility for the effect of our aggressiveness as it intersects with our social and professional power and status. This point is implied by my third observation above, but deserves special treatment because of its importance. We have observed that wounded aggressiveness results in, for example, excessive introversion, failure of connection, ego-weakness, and insufficient healthy narcissism. To have a healthy relationship to our aggressiveness, or to be successful in repairing the wounds caused in our aggressiveness by trauma, means that we are likely to possess or have gained certain personality qualities, for example, greater extroversion and charisma, self-assurance and self-confidence, relative ease with our influence and exercise of power. These qualities are not necessarily violent or abusive, as our study has made clear. But we have not cultivated a mature enough relationship to aggression until we embody qualities like these with an acute sensitivity to how our professional or other social power can inflate and distort even constructive aggressive qualities. In combination, aggressiveness and professional stature are often perceived as, and too easily become, manipulative and even violent. For example, the kinds of qualities inherent in healthy aggressiveness are very closely aligned with popular or at least traditional hallmarks of an effective ministry: charisma, confidence, and influence. The majority of ministers and other religious leaders use such qualities nonviolently. But it has also been shown that religious leaders who are abusers often use characteristics like personal charisma to gain the trust of people in their care and then violate them.[3] Maturity in regard to aggressiveness requires religious professionals to embody such characteristics not mindlessly but with finely tuned sensitivity: some people have been abused through such qualities and may be disconcerted by a pastor's charisma, confidence, and power, however constructively embodied. Religious communities evidence maturity regarding aggression when they are analytical about the aggressiveness of their leaders and engage intentionally in collaboration with their leaders in the ethical exercise of aggressiveness.

Finally, our expression of aggression has flowered into maturity when, acknowledging the real and potential destructiveness of our own aggression, we tend to be restrained with our use of it to tear things down (verbally and otherwise) and tend to be generous with our use of it to help repair that which has been destroyed. When we use our aggressiveness exclusively, or even primarily for critique, it is likely we will contribute unnecessarily to violence.

Aggression and Spiritual Practice

In light of the reflections in previous chapters, it is clear that the ambiguity and relationality of aggression presents significant challenge to some religious formulations. Though religion has to do with binding up, as the etymology of the word suggests, we have seen that aggression often propels us into breaking loose of those things that bind us. While most religious communities have focused on the regulation of impulse and intimacy, aggression floods us with spontaneity and lustiness. Where spiritual practices favor breaking down barriers and freeing pent-up emotion, aggression is often reason and means by which to set boundaries on expression and contact. Yet, spiritual and religious life not infrequently evolve as arenas to which people turn to wrestle with both the wreckage and worth of aggressive power. Spiritual practice is one means by which we can cultivate resources to care for aggression in trauma, healing, and maturation. Though we can barely scratch the surface of the issues relating aggression and spiritual practice, the reflections of previous chapters bring a few issues into sharp relief.

First, because aggression exists, is not optional, and is a frequently satisfying, pleasurable form of power, caring for aggression in spiritual practice means taking advantage of the opportunity it affords for stark honesty about aggression: "the soul loves power."[4] Our souls hunger for the experience of capability, influence, and passion, to which we have partial access through our aggressiveness. Yes, we must attend in spiritual practice to our capacity to *misuse* our power, and we will turn to that shortly. However, in light of our theological conviction that human power was created in sacredness and declared good, it is spiritually essential to care for our souls' *love* of power to at least an equal extent. There are few contexts or relationships where it is appropriate to honestly admit the secret but bald pleasure we get from the adult equivalents of childhood omnipotence: being right, excellent, authoritative, noticed, or financially solvent, for example. In most contexts it is considered bad manners to speak of this reality. But in private spiritual practice this reality cannot and need not be concealed: after all, we were created for and with power. In the privacy of prayer and other spiritual disciplines, we can bring out and enjoy this gift given to us at our creation without the unnecessarily guilty conscience that can plague even our constructive expressions of aggression. God's capacity to survive our aggressiveness reminds us that our love of power is not inherently sinful.

We deny our soul's love of power at our own peril and also at risk to others. If denied the direct and useful exercise of power, the soul often accomplishes it surreptitiously, and with less guidance and control from one's conscious values. Thus religious people who claim an excess of humility and servanthood almost inevitably commit violence and the manipulations of passive aggression. Perhaps even more familiar is the vacuity of religious people who have sought to deny the soul's yearning for power. "People feel empty more than uncontrollably aggressive. Our task is to help put the spirit back in the soul."[5]

Second, caring for aggression in spiritual practice means that we must pray our aggression. Prayer and some other forms of meditative practice can be one of the contexts in which we re-parent our aggressiveness—gifting ourselves with a bit of primary preoccupation (retreat, for example) and potential space (guided meditation, for example) in which to play around and become acquainted with aggressiveness in the imaginative and yet relatively safe context of prayerful spiritual disciplines. The sacred sanctuary of prayer and meditation—love, repentance, forgiveness, grace—can go a long way toward repairing the wounds inflicted on aggression by trauma. The connection, power, and affirmation of prayer can, over time, fill in the gaps of failure to connect, lack of ego-strength, and lack of healthy narcissism.

But neither is the value of spiritual practice found in perfect satisfaction of our needs, and in prayer we should be prepared immediately to encounter failures in aggression—most everyday, some perhaps traumatic. Do we really want to know our aggression? Why would we want to curb the exhilaration we feel when we lord it over others? What good does it do to rehearse all the situations in which we should have acted or spoken, and did not? Do we really want to feel our fury toward God, toward the church, or toward those who hold power in it? And we meet frighteningly opposite sides of ourselves. In their book on prayer, Ann and Barry Ulanov include a highly valuable chapter on the interplay between aggressivity and prayer. Their account is so descriptive, even evocative, of the actual experience of aggression's challenging ambiguity and relationality that it is worthwhile to quote it at some length.

> Prayer makes it impossible to avoid aggression. We notice how irritable we are, how hard to please, how easily made discontented, jumpy, nervous, quarrelsome. We are full of restless, unchanneled energy, turning back on itself. Gusts of vigorous emotion confront us, ready to be lived, but we do not know where or how. Surges of determination and extreme resolutions burst through in prayer, as if we had suddenly discovered wild horses living in our house, kicking to get out, horses that need to be ridden, guided and enjoyed. . . .
>
> On the other hand, our aggression may show itself in an opposite way, in diffused form. We do not know what we think or feel. We flop about, unwilling to make decisions. We hope others will do something that will decide an issue for us. We talk our insights or possibilities away, parking them on others instead of working on them ourselves. We show aggressiveness by the way we drift along, half-clear, half-determined, half-decided, until everyone around us is ready to scream at us because of our refusal to coagulate or to act.[6]

Many of us find it difficult to hold to the prayer disciplines that we desire. If "praying opens up our aggression,"[7] the confounding realities of aggression being what they are, perhaps one reason we avoid prayer is to avoid our aggression. However, if violence is to be decreased, and if vitality is to be found for building up the realm of God on earth, there is no way around this: we must pray our aggression.

The privacy of personal prayer offers private space in which to cultivate necessary honesty about our aggression and to seek to make reparation for any offenses we have committed with it. This is similar to two of the twelve steps of Alcoholics Anonymous: taking "a fearless and searching inventory of ourselves" and making "amends" to all those we have harmed.[8] This involves identifying and taking steps to remedy the distortions in our aggressiveness: our most obvious violences, the subtlest ways in which we contribute to the vicious circle of contempt discussed in chapter 2, the ways in which we allow passivity to diffuse our identity and witness. Then, we go a step further in moral inventory. We mine our aggression for its every bit of contribution toward sustaining us for fighting evil and repairing the brokenness in our world. We identify and begin to polish all the areas in which we have been able to use our aggressiveness constructively, or could. We concentrate on identifying particular areas of strength, focus, and achievement and on using those areas as media through which to make a constructively aggressive contribution to the betterment of the world. At the same time, caring for aggression in prayer rubs away any hubris that we have about our capacity to be in full control of our aggressiveness or put pure goodness where creation has installed multivalence. Honesty in prayer makes our kinship with Cain plain. We know that any differences between our aggressive behavior and Cain's cannot be attributed to fundamental differences in our natures.

Periods of unavoidable suffering, not knowing, and disillusionment provide another opportunity to pray our aggression.[9] If we are willing to venture deeply into these times with both our prayer and our aggressivity, we will create the perseverance that enables us, somehow, to endure and even more, with God, to "make a way out of no way."[10] How do we pray our aggression in hard times? This is the most difficult and yet straightforward challenge. We hang on for dear life. We stubbornly refuse to quit or to give in to despair or evil. In faith, we keep putting one foot in front of the other. And we refuse to minimize the magnificence of this simple aggressivity. Aggression shimmers in us as a grace-filled focus and unstoppable determination.

Prayer regularly pursued is rich with images and visions, and this provides yet another means of praying our aggression. Biblical images provide richly familiar catalysts for increasing the imaginativeness with which we are able to pray aggression. Mark 9:49–50, for example, picturesquely notes that everyone is "salted with fire," made a bit briny from life's sufferings, and that the challenge is to simultaneously "have salt in yourselves, and be at peace with one another." Meditation on these images might enable us to respond affirmatively to the call (stated also in Matthew 5:13 and Luke 14:34) to maintain one's saltiness peacefully, to flavor but not overwhelm corporate life. This combination—being salty and at the same time peaceful—is arguably a summons to constructive aggressiveness.

Additionally, we can seek to open ourselves to new ideas and feelings toward aggression that might come unbidden during nondirective forms of meditation like centering prayer. Or we can intentionally seek to exercise and condition our aggressivity through visualization or guided meditation. Still other possibilities for the cultivation of greater comfort with aggression are provided in more physical forms of prayer, like Zen walking meditation. In all these ways, prayer provides us imaginative space where seeds of notions about aggression's values can be coaxed into development, a bit apart from the complexity of actual encounter with others.

Finally, praying our aggression is space to cultivate the courage to embody aggression in the world in nondominant, creative ways. The Ulanovs put it this way: "Aggression allowed in prayer equips us to risk being foolish for God, makes us willing to look ridiculous in public, and allows us to go with what we believe. We discover the nerve to fail in the service of a daring loyalty to the God who has touched us."[11]

Spiritual practice provides a third means of caring for aggression: care for the body and thus honoring and cultivating the physiological roots of aggression. While it would also have been appropriate while discussing the healing and maturation of aggression to discuss caring for aggression through care of the body, I place the discussion here to emphasize that care of the body and its aggressiveness is a spiritual urgency. Poor stewardship of our physical energies— lack of use, care, or caution in regard to use of our bodies—afflicts too many of us. We have a responsibility to develop a constructive relationship with our bodies through which we become knowledgeable about its powers and vulnerabilities. From this point of view, exercise is no more optional to care of the body than food or sleep. Without knowing our bodies, we have little chance of discovering our aggression at all, much less turning it to ethical employments. Because aggression so often is expressed through violent physicality, aggression's relationship to the body may at first glance seem largely dangerous.

But it is also important to note that a positive relationship with our bodies— in exercise, gardening, dance, teaching, yoga, movement of nearly any kind— often reveals to us and fosters in us an increased, positive, and pleasurable sense of our powerfulness. In spirited, leisure movement, we can play around with aggressiveness, and develop greater comfort, control, and confidence in its value. From this new position, we help to reduce the caricature of the body as a seething cauldron of wild and uncontrollable passions and experience it instead as a fount of energy which can be delightful or agitating, but which in either case begs for employment and expression. From this point of view, aggression helps us foster a more holistic and healthy relationship to the body and appreciate in a new way its sacredness.

Disciplined use of our bodies seems to increase our ability to experience and utilize aggressiveness in life-affirming directions. For example, athletics, not infrequently experienced by participants as a spiritual discipline, has helped young girls develop and use aggressiveness in constructive ways. A *Newsweek* article reporting on the expected dominance of women athletes at the 1996 Summer

Olympics cites research that shows that girls who are involved in athletics do better in academics and are less likely to take drugs or become pregnant. This early playing around with aggressiveness seems tied to later personal achievement (and competition): "A full eighty percent of women in key positions in the Fortune 500 identify themselves as erstwhile 'tomboys.'"[12]

A fourth arena where aggression can be cared for through spiritual practice is in corporate religious life. First, the silence in religious communities about aggression can be—and needs to be—broken. Aggression and its variety of manifestations should be gotten on the table as an explicit topic of conversation. Related to this is a second issue: we lack theologies sufficient to undergird the development of a healthy spirituality of aggression. The breaking of silence about aggression might well include a congregation's explicit conversation about difficult theological issues in aggression. We need, for example, more explicitly stated theologies of self-defense. Because of the traditional Christian emphasis on service, sacrifice, and personal sin, few of us have participated in discussion of what might be reasonable theological grounds for setting limits on emotional aggressiveness used against us, self-defense against verbal violence. This is of special concern since the expression of violent aggressiveness is almost always caused in part by the feeling of threat and a person's felt need for self-defense.

An especially rich arena of congregational life where we can care for aggression is in collective nonviolent resistance and other forms of activism. Collective activism provides a valuable relational context for aggressive action and, potentially, the accountability of relationship. Spiritual disciplines offer a multitude of ways that faithful people can lend nonviolent but direct, vigorous action on behalf of important issues in church and society. The power of aggression can be a source of the grit, pertinacity, courage, and ingeniousness required to resist evil. We must underline a danger here, however. Too often, aggressive activism is nothing more than self-righteousness, judgmentalism, and guilt-production. This use of aggression is abusive, seldom transformative, and sometimes counterproductive. Fingerpointing continues the cycle of violence and risks increasing the danger and intractability of oppressors' behavior. To be constructive and energizing, aggression must do more than simply identify and resist aggression. Aggression is much more spiritually valuable when it goes further and helps repair the damages done by evil. Aggression's main value in activism is its capacity to fuel the recognition of our personal responsibility for evil and our own energetic engagement in setting things right.

Aggression and Conflict

As we consider what it means to care for aggression in the context of conflict, two main points are immediately preeminent. First, to the degree that we have not cared for our aggressiveness before finding ourselves in a conflict, we will be more likely to function violently in the conflict. Second, because very few of us have had sufficient parenting regarding constructive aggression, conflicts often become occasions for offering to one another the simple but priceless gift of surviving—with a minimum of traumatic failure—each other's nonviolent aggression.

Our study of aggression makes clear that conflict is an inevitable and not necessarily negative aspect of life together. Several insights fan out from aggression's is-ness. Aggression will happen, and it often will lead to conflict. The innateness of aggression in each person, its often fierce materialization of the life force, the prevalence of threat and violence in the world, the frequency with which aggressiveness is provoked as defense, and the way in which aggressive expression can seem to crowd relationship—all these factors suggest the close relationship between aggression and conflict. Thus it is not helpful to ignore or resist or denigrate conflict categorically.

The wide range of aggressive expression that we have been considering also suggests that we all participate in conflict, whether we do so with silence or words, with action or inaction. Aloofness in conflict says as much as active participation, though it might be harder to decipher. Those responsible for oversight in a situation of conflict must engage both passive and active participants if the conflict is to be understood and resolved. But as participants in a situation of conflict, spiritual maturity is evidenced by our capacity to monitor ourselves. If we are inclined to aggressive expression, we are obligated to restrain our aggressiveness enough to make substantial room for others. It is not the responsibility of others to elbow their way into conversation. Then again, if we are inclined toward nonaggressiveness, we are obligated to assert ourselves. It is not the responsibility of others to coerce us to speak.[13] Additionally, our study of aggression helps identify why it can help defuse a conflict to admit the value in the other person's position: hostile aggression is so often expressed because a person feels threatened, and conflicts in aggression are not resolved except in the validating context of relationship, validation of an opponents' views can reduce the sense of threat and be a first step toward the respectful relationship required for conflict resolution.

An additional point suggested by our study of aggression's violence is that we must take responsibility for the violence that can so easily seep into conflict. When we aggressively communicate an idea we have or the feeling that we have been wronged, our confrontation of others can slip into abusiveness. One of the downsides of the contemporary attention to the value of anger is that some of us have come to believe that having a right to our anger means that we also have a right to express it in any way we please and that those who love us are obligated to accept our modes of angry expression as a sign of their love for us and acceptance of our feelings. The relationality of aggression makes clear that this is a fallacy. We must take responsibility for the manner in which we express our aggression, however justified, because to fail to do so contaminates the safety of relational space and potentially inhibits or embitters the other's aggressive expression.

As we have seen, caring for aggression is demanding, tough work. It does not come naturally; it can and must be proactively taught. One implication here is that every community could care for aggression and likely decrease violence by providing affordable, convenient, and regular access to training in conflict mediation or resolution and in nonviolence training. Many denominations and religious resource organizations have trained staff members ready to provide such instruction, and to do so with attention to religious and spiritual foundations and implications. Conflict mediation training could be required of all committee chairpersons in a congregation or other organization. Similarly, conflict resolution is a part of any adequate training for parents and others involved in the guidance of children. The regular provision of such training is another way to communicate several important factors about aggression: conflict happens, is normal, and can be healthy; there is no shame in coming for training in that everyone needs education and support in managing their aggressiveness in relation to conflict; there are helpful and harmful ways of being aggressive; and individuals must take responsibility for their aggression.

The kinship of love and aggression highlights another issue in approaching conflict: we must speak the truth, but with love. We must confront, but with compassion. Theologian Andrew Sung Park discusses the necessity for compassionate confrontation of oppressors in the resolution of *han,* the depth of human suffering.

> Confrontation without understanding will cause unnecessary, hostile conflict. Compassion without confrontation will result in ineffective transformation. Confrontation with the heart of compassion for the oppressors will genuinely change their heart through creative tension.[14]

This sounds a lot like Martin Luther King, Jr.'s, contention that the "creative tension" between tough-mindedness and tenderheartedness would convert racist oppressors.[15] But how can this stance be found and maintained? The key to compassionate confrontation is found in the understanding that confrontation of others always includes self-confrontation[16]: we accept that we are not immune to the evil, sin, or error we experience in others' actions. Having no self-righteousness, we are more able to have empathy for the other's human limitation. Knowing that this sin, or one equally grievous, is surely ours, we strive to confront the other as we wish to be confronted.[17] One crucial way to increase our ability to confront in these ways is to work actively not only on identifying and accepting our anger but also on practicing the constructive expression of it.[18]

Our study of aggression suggests that we have not given enough attention to cultivating the ability to survive necessary conflict, to be confronted when wrong, and to receive justifiable criticism. One sign of the prevalence of the failure to rally constructively aggressive energies can be seen in the widespread feeling of fragility in the face of conflict. Even when the conflict is fair, even when the confrontation is compassionate, many people have little capacity to listen, acknowledge, and set about repairing the wrong done. Two responses are common instead: vociferous denial or self-crushing guilt.

Evelyn and James Whitehead identify three attitudes that are essential for healthy assertion, which is, as noted previously, a form of aggressiveness: self-awareness, self-disclosure, and self-worth.[19] I suggest these attitudes are, as well, the emotional reserves out of which comes the ability to be resilient in the face of conflict and open to compassionate confrontation. Their cultivation is an essential part of using one's aggression for the purposes of building one's effectiveness as a human being and as a participant in conflict. *Self-awareness* is "an ability to know where I am now, to be in touch with the dense and ambiguous information of my own life,"[20] and enables one to monitor one's feelings and responses in the moment of conflict. *Self-disclosure* is the cultivated ability to express concretely and accurately one's ideas, needs, and purposes,[21] which, in conflict, means that one has the words to express one's reactions and reality. *Self-worth,* arguably the foundation of the other two abilities, is the belief that one's ideas, feelings, and self are valuable and deserve to be received with respect and seriousness not only by others but also by oneself.[22] In the midst of confrontation, self-worth enables us to remember that, even with our limitations and failings, we are people of value.

Neither compassionate confrontation nor cultivation of the ability to receive confrontation less defensively will make conflict easy. The ambiguity and relationality of aggression make that an impossible dream. But attention to both makes it more possible that we will survive each other's aggressiveness and experience in the aftermath of conflict a precious seasoning of relationship.

Epilogue

We convert, if we do at all, not by demanding something impossible, but by being something irresistible.

—May Sarton

Nothing is so strong as gentleness; nothing so gentle as real strength.

—Attributed to St. Francis de Sales

I WONDER—Are our explorations here one more demand for the impossible? Have our explorations awakened any possibility that, with practice and patience, we could gradually nurture aggressiveness into a collective vitality irresistible enough to convert us to the power of nonviolence?

I *am* sure that few things in the world are more irresistible than gentle strength and strong gentleness. Perhaps aggression—reckoned with, re-braided with love, and well cared for—will yield them both.

Notes

Notes to the Introduction

1. "Dear Jesus, In Whose Life I See," in *The United Methodist Hymnal: Book of United Methodist Worship* (Nashville: The United Methodist Publishing House, 1989), 468.
2. I prefer to use the term *culture* in its broadest sense, "the sum total of ways of living developed by a group of human beings to meet biological and psychosocial needs" (see Elaine Pinderhughes, *Understanding Race, Ethnicity and Power: The Key to Efficacy in Clinical Practice* [New York: Free Press, 1989], 6). Aspects of identity such as ethnicity, nationality, sex, and religion form subcultures within this broader rubric.
3. For further discussion of feminist pastoral theological method, see, for example, Valerie M. DeMarinis, *Critical Caring: A Feminist Model for Pastoral Psychology* (Louisville: Westminster/John Knox Press, 1993), 17–19.
4. Psychologist and Jesuit priest Ignacio Martín-Baró, who was assassinated with five other priests and two women by government soldiers in El Salvador in November 1989, discussed liberation as a criterion for the effectiveness of any discipline that claims to serve individual or collective good. See Martín-Baró, *Writings for a Liberation Psychology,* ed. Adrianne Aron and Shawn Corne (Cambridge, Mass.: Harvard University Press, 1994).
5. For further discussion of pastoral theological method, especially the crucial aspect of its systemic approach, see Larry Kent Graham, *Care of Persons, Care of Worlds: A Psychosystems Approach to Pastoral Care and Counseling* (Nashville: Abingdon Press, 1992).
6. "Aggression," in *Merriam-Webster's Collegiate Dictionary,* 10th ed. (Springfield, Mass.: Merriam-Webster, Inc. 1995).
7. I sometimes include references to this range of emotions and behaviors in our study, since it is my contention that they imply aggression. But since this book is a study of aggression, not of specific forms of aggression such as anger or conflict, I favor explicit references to aggression where they are available.

8. Marjorie Hewitt Suchocki, *The Fall to Violence: Original Sin in Relational Theology* (New York: Continuum, 1994), 85.

9. See, for example, Anne Bathurst Gilson, *Eros Breaking Free: Interpreting Sexual Theo-Ethics* (Cleveland: Pilgrim Press, 1995); Carter Heyward, *Touching Our Strength: The Erotic as Power and the Love of God* (New York: Harper & Row, 1989); Audre Lorde, "Uses of the Erotic: The Erotic as Power," in *Sister Outsider: Essays and Speeches* (Trumansburg, N.Y.: Crossing Press, 1984); James B. Nelson, *Body Theology* (Louisville, Ky.: Westminster/John Knox Press, 1992).

10. Bonnie J. Miller-McLemore, *Also a Mother: Work and Family as Theological Dilemma* (Nashville: Abingdon Press, 1994), 13.

Notes to Chapter 1.
Problems in Aggression

1. The concepts of "experience-near" and "experience-distant" theory are developed by Heinz Kohut in *How Does Analysis Cure?* ed. Arnold Goldberg (Chicago: University of Chicago Press, 1984), 186–87. These notions correspond roughly to first-order and second-order religious language. Compare T. W. Jennings, Jr., "Pastoral Theological Methodology," in *Dictionary of Pastoral Care and Counseling,* ed. Rodney J. Hunter (Nashville: Abingdon Press, 1990), 862.

2. Kohut, *How Does Analysis Cure?* 186–87.

3. This slogan was originated by the Fellowship of Reconciliation.

4. Cited in Alexander Abdennur, *The Conflict Resolution Syndrome: Volunteerism, Violence, and Beyond* (Ottawa: University of Ottawa Press, 1987), 117. I am grateful to Mark Carver for bringing this quote to my attention.

5. Marjorie Hewitt Suchocki, *The Fall to Violence: Original Sin in Relational Theology* (New York: Continuum, 1994), 95.

6. Eleanor Randolph, "Were Fired Reporters Too Aggressive?" *Los Angeles Times,* 17 February 1996, A21.

7. Nancy J. Ramsay, "Sexual Abuse and Shame: The Travail of Recovery," in *Women in Travail and Transition: A New Pastoral Care,* ed. Maxine Glaz and Jeanne Stevenson Moessner (Minneapolis: Fortress Press, 1991), 111.

8. Abuse is not limited to interpersonal violence, like sexual violence. Social and structural violence—such as racism and homophobia—are also abusive.

9. Margaret R. Miles, *Practicing Christianity: Critical Perspectives for an Embodied Spirituality* (New York: Crossroad, 1990), 3.

10. Susan Nelson Dunfee, "The Sin of Hiding: A Feminist Critique of Reinhold Niebuhr's Account of the Sin of Pride," *Soundings* 45 (Fall 1982): 320.

11. See Melanie Klein, "Notes on Some Schizoid Mechanisms," in *Envy and Gratitude and Other Works 1946–1963,* vol. 3: *The Writings of Melanie Klein* (New York: Free Press, 1975).

12. In extreme situations of trauma, splitting is "walling off" from conscious awareness wounded parts of the psyche, by "leaving" the body, or by acting out different and unintegrated personalities or personality qualities. See Ellen Bass and Laura Davis, *The Courage to Heal* (New York: Harper & Row, 1988), 209–10.

13. Suchocki, *The Fall to Violence,* 53.

14. I consider this issue more fully in Kathleen J. Greider, "The Authority of Our

Ambivalence: Women and Priestly Ministry," *Quarterly Review* 10 (Winter 1990): 22–39.

15. Clinical illustrations come from my private practice as a pastoral counselor and are compilations or are otherwise disguised for the purpose of confidentiality.

16. The maturation of ambivalence and its relationship to aggression in childhood is discussed in Henri Parens, "Developmental Considerations of Ambivalence," *Psychoanalytic Study of the Child* 34 (1979):385–420. On the role of "the ambiguous self" in adults healing from trauma, see James Newton Poling, *The Abuse of Power: A Theological Problem* (Nashville: Abingdon Press, 1991), 110–18. For a sociological reading of the value of ambivalence, see Andrew J. Weigert, *Mixed Emotions: Certain Steps toward Understanding Ambivalence* (Albany: State University of New York Press, 1991).

17. Robert Kegan, *The Evolving Self: Problem and Process in Human Development* (Cambridge, Mass.: Harvard University Press, 1982), 44.

18. Simone de Beauvoir, *The Ethics of Ambiguity,* trans. Bernard Frechtman (New York: Philosophical Library, 1948), 133.

19. Suchocki, *The Fall to Violence,* 53.

20. Weigert, *Mixed Emotions,* 32.

21. Judith V. Jordan, Alexandra G. Kaplan, Jean Baker Miller et al.: *Women's Growth in Connection: Writings from the Stone Center* (New York: Guilford Press, 1991), 61.

22. Object relations theory, self-in-relation theory, and systems theories are examples. Increasing emphasis on couple, family, and group care also evidences this trend.

23. Murray Bowen, *Family Therapy in Clinical Practice* (New York: Jason Aronson, · 1978), 198–99.

24. For discussion of an "ecological self," see Joanna Macy, "Awakening to the Ecological Self," in *Healing the Wounds: The Promise of Ecofeminism,* ed. Judith Plant (Toronto: Between the Lines, 1989), 201–11.

25. Sallie McFague, *Models of God: Theology for an Ecological, Nuclear Age* (Minneapolis: Fortress Press, 1987), 69–78.

26. Examples of works that capture what I see as major characteristics and strengths of depth psychological approaches to aggression include Melanie Klein, "Love, Guilt and Reparation," in *Love, Guilt and Reparation and Other Works 1921–1945,* vol. 1: *The Writings of Melanie Klein* (New York: Free Press, 1975); Heinz Kohut, "Thoughts on Narcissism and Narcissistic Rage," in *The Search for the Self: Selected Writings of Heinz Kohut 1950–1978,* vol. 2, ed. Paul Ornstein (New York: International Universities Press, 1978); Ana-Maria Rizzuto, Jerome I. Sashin, Dan H. Buie, and W. W. Meissner, "A Revised Theory of Aggression," *Psychoanalytic Review* 80 (Spring 1993): 29–54; Anthony Storr, *Human Aggression* (New York: Atheneum, 1968); Donald W. Winnicott, *Deprivation and Delinquency,* ed. Clare Winnicott, Ray Shepherd, and Madeleine Davis (London: Tavistock Publishers, 1984).

27. Clara Thompson, *Interpersonal Psychoanalysis,* ed. Maurice Green (New York: Basic Books, 1964), 179.

28. Ibid.

29. D. W. Winnicott, *Through Paediatrics to Psychoanalysis,* ed. Masud R. Khan (New York: Basic Books, 1975), 204.

30. Jean Baker Miller, *Toward a New Psychology of Women,* rev. ed. (Boston: Beacon Press, 1986), 115–16.

31. Though it was not his first opinion about aggression, in his writings after the First World War, Freud gave destructiveness the stature of a drive, variously calling it a death drive, an aggressive drive, and a drive toward destructiveness. For a thorough review of Freud's aggression theory see Paul E. Stepansky, *A History of Aggression in Freud* (New York: International Universities Press, 1977). Though most psychoanalysts quickly disputed the possibility of a death drive, Melanie Klein was one of the few theorists who pursued the notion of the death instinct (Klein, *Envy and Gratitude*).

32. For example, see Erich Fromm, *The Anatomy of Human Destructiveness* (New York: Holt, Rinehart & Winston, 1973); Rollo May, *Power and Innocence: A Search for the Sources of Violence* (New York: W. W. Norton & Co, 1972). For a helpful review of psychoanalytic theories of aggression that shows their emphasis on destructiveness, see Peter Gay, *The Cultivation of Hatred,* vol. 3: *The Bourgeois Experience: Victoria to Freud* (New York: W. W. Norton & Co., 1993), 529–36.

33. Otto Kernberg is one contemporary proponent of this view. See his book, *Object Relations Theory and Clinical Psychoanalysis* (New York: Jason Aronson, 1976).

34. In 1986, a group of twenty leading scientists from around the world produced the widely quoted Seville Statement on Violence in which they dispute "alleged biological findings that have been used . . . to justify violence and war." Specifically, they concurred that "it is scientifically incorrect to say that": (1) we have inherited from our animal ancestors a tendency to make war; (2) any violent behavior is genetically programmed into human nature; (3) in the course of evolution, there has been a selection for aggressive behavior more than for any other behavior; (4) humans have a violent "brain"; (5) war is caused by instinct or any single motivation. These researchers have established only that there is no instinct or drive to violence in human beings, however, not that there is no aggressive instinct or drive. For commentary and the full text of the Seville Statement, see David Adams, "The Seville Statement on Violence: A Progress Report," *Journal of Peace Research* 26 (1989): 113–21.

35. For a discussion of these issues in more depth, see Jane Flax, *Thinking Fragments: Psychoanalysis, Feminism, and Postmodernism in the Contemporary West* (Berkeley: University of California Press, 1990), 90, 108, 120–26.

36. The definition used by social psychologist and widely quoted aggression researcher Leonard Berkowitz is typical: Aggression is "any behavior that is intended to harm someone physically or psychologically" (Berkowitz, *Aggression: Its Causes, Consequences, and Control* [Philadelphia: Temple University Press, 1993], 3).

37. Representatives of a social psychological approach to aggression studies include Leonard Berkowitz, *Aggression: A Social Psychological Analysis* (New York: McGraw-Hill, 1962); L. D. Eron, "The Development of Aggressive Behavior from the Perspective of a Developing Behaviorism," *American Psychologist* 42 (May 1987): 435–42; L. Rowell Huesmann, ed., *Aggressive Behavior: Current Perspectives* (New York: Plenum Press, 1994).

38. John Dollard, Leonard W. Doob, Neal E. Miller et al., *Frustration and Aggression* (New Haven: Yale University Press, 1939).

39. Albert Bandura, *Aggression: A Social Learning Analysis* (Englewood Cliffs, N.J.: Prentice-Hall, 1973).

40. L. D. Eron, "Theories of Aggression: From Drives to Cognitions," in Huesmann, ed., *Aggressive Behavior,* 7–9.

41. Arnold P. Goldstein, *The Ecology of Aggression* (New York: Plenum Press, 1994).
42. Representatives of contemporary cross-cultural, ethnological, and anthropological approaches include Victoria Katherine Burbank, *Fighting Women: Anger and Aggression in Aboriginal Australia* (Berkeley: University of California Press, 1994); Arnold P. Goldstein and Marshall H. Segall, eds., *Aggression in Global Perspective* (New York: Pergamon Press, 1983); David Levinson, *Family Violence in Cross-Cultural Perspective* (Newbury Park, Calif.: Sage Publications, 1989).
43. See, for example, Berkowitz, *Aggression: Its Causes, Consequences, and Control*, 6.
44. The divergence between academic and popular meanings of aggression is intriguing. It is as if popular language reveals a fairly balanced ego position in regard to aggression, while aggression's bad reputation in formal thought is more a superego position vis-à-vis aggression. The equation of aggression with violence may reflect our conscious, scholarly, dominant, doctrinal point of view. But it ignores the more unconscious, popular, subordinated, and spiritual point of view, which is that aggression is sometimes necessary and valuable and not so harmful. I am grateful to Carroll Saussy for her help in developing this point.
45. For example, Berkowitz says that he uses *violence* only to refer to "an extreme form of aggression, a deliberate attempt to do serious physical harm" (Berkowitz, *Aggression: Its Causes, Consequences, and Control*, 11).
46. "[Laboratory] procedures generally are only a pale reflection of real-life hostile interactions; the frustrations they employ usually are relatively mild, and the aggressive reactions typically are fairly tame" (Leonard Berkowitz, *Aggression: Its Causes, Consequences, and Control*, x). The same can be true for field-based observational studies; many people seek to restrain their worst violences if they think they might be observed.
47. A. L. Edwards, *The Social Desirability Variable in Personality Assessment and Research* (New York: Dryden, 1957).
48. There are two exceptions to this critique. Two recent volumes on the relationship between gender and aggression are multidisciplinary in scope: Kaj Björkqvist and Pirkko Niemelä, eds., *Of Mice and Women: Aspects of Female Aggression* (San Diego: Academic Press, 1992); John Archer, ed., *Male Violence* (London: Routledge, 1994). Also, social interactionist theory is self-consciously attempting to bridge the gap between disciplines in aggression studies. See Richard B. Felson and James T. Tedeschi, eds., *Aggression and Violence: Social Interactionist Approaches* (Washington, D.C.: American Psychological Association, 1993).
49. Kirsti M. J. Lagerspetz and Kaj Björkqvist, "Indirect Aggression in Girls and Boys," in Huesmann, ed. *Aggressive Behavior*. See also Kaj Björkqvist, Karin Österman, and Ari Kaukiainen, "The Development of Direct and Indirect Aggressive Strategies in Males and Females," in Björkqvist and Niemelä, eds., *Of Mice and Women*.
50. Dennis J. Kutzer, "Psychobiological Factors in Violent Behavior," in *Assessment and Intervention*, vol. 1: *Violent Behavior*, ed. Leonard J. Hertzberg, Gene F. Ostrum, and Joan Roberts Field (Great Neck, N.Y.: PMA Publishing Co., 1990), 29–40.
51. Ibid., 27.
52. Leonard Berkowitz, "On the Formation and Regulation of Anger and Aggression: A Cognitive-Neoassociationistic Analysis," *American Psychologist* 45 (April 1990): 498.

53. Eleanor Emmons Maccoby and Carol Nagy Jacklin, *The Psychology of Sex Differences* (Stanford, Calif.: Stanford University Press, 1974), 243–46.

54. Natalie Angier, "Does Testosterone Equal Aggression? Maybe Not," *New York Times,* 20 June 1995. Perhaps even more surprising, after testosterone replacement therapy, the men reported an increase in their feelings of optimism and friendliness. These results are in keeping with recent findings in other laboratories.

55. Thomas H. Maugh II, "Study Says Lead Exposure May Contribute to Crime," *Los Angeles Times,* 7 February 1996, A1.

56. K. O. Christensen, "The Genesis of Aggressive Criminality: Implications of a Study of Crime in a Danish Twin Study," in *Determinants and Origins of Aggressive Behavior,* ed. J. De Wit and W. W. Hartup (The Hague: Mouton, 1974), 233–53.

57. Donald S. Williamson, "A Study of Selective Inhibition of Aggression by Church Members," *Journal of Pastoral Care* 21 (December 1967): 194–95.

58. David W. Augsburger, "Anger and Aggression," in *Clinical Handbook of Pastoral Counseling,* vol. 1, exp. ed., ed. Robert J. Wicks, Richard D. Parsons, and Donald Capps (New York: Paulist Press, 1993), 482–87. See also Augsburger, *Conflict Mediation across Cultures: Pathways and Patterns* (Louisville, Ky.: Westminster John Knox Press, 1995), 117–119.

59. Augsburger, "Anger and Aggression," 484. Augsburger is not the only pastoral psychologist to define aggression negatively. The major reference work for the discipline of pastoral care and counseling also emphasizes aggression's connection to harmful behavior: "Aggression is a form of behavior in which persons express their rights, thoughts, and feelings without regard for the rights, thoughts, and feelings of other persons" (R. K. Sanders, "Aggression and Assertion," in Hunter, ed., *Dictionary of Pastoral Care and Counseling,* 14). Morton T. Kelsey emphasizes the connection between aggression and destructive tendencies in "Aggression and Religion: The Psychology and Theology of the Punitive Element in Man," *Religious Education* 68 (May–June 1973): 366–86.

60. Augsburger, "Anger and Aggression," 494.

61. In addition to sources already cited, see David W. Augsburger, *Caring Enough to Confront: The Love-Fight* (Scottdale, Pa.: Herald Press, 1973); David W. Augsburger, *Anger and Assertiveness in Pastoral Care* (Philadelphia: Fortress Press, 1979).

62. For example, in one place, Augsburger says that aggression is the physical expression of anger ("Anger and Aggression," 482). In another, he seems to say that the roots of conflict lie in aggression (*Conflict Meditation,* 117).

63. Suchocki, *The Fall to Violence,* 82–99.

64. Mohandas K. Gandhi, *Non-Violent Resistance (Satyagraha)* (New York: Schocken Books, 1961), 175.

65. Martin Luther King, Jr., "Nonviolence and Racial Justice," in *A Testament of Hope: The Essential Writings and Speeches of Martin Luther King, Jr.,* ed. James M. Washington (San Francisco: HarperCollins, 1986), 7.

66. Roger Steenland, "Our Aggression," *The Reformed Review* 20 (March 1967): 70–72; Williamson, "A Study of Selective Inhibition," 1967; Joachim Illies, "Aggression and Evil: Meditation on the Biology of the Fall of Man," *Concurrence* 1 (Fall 1969):296–306; Everett R. Clinchy, "The Moral Equivalent to Aggression," *Zygon* 4 (1969):238–50; the editorial and all five articles of the September 1971 issue of *Pastoral Psychology* (vol. 22), which were devoted to "aggression and violence";

W. W. Meissner, "Toward a Theology of Human Aggression," *Journal of Religion and Health* 10 (October 1971):324–32; Robert C. Williams, "Moral Suasion and Militant Aggression in the Theological Perspective of Black Religion," *Journal of Religious Thought* 30 (Fall–Winter 1973–74): 27–50.

67. Konrad Lorenz, *On Aggression* (London: Methuen, 1966).

68. Meissner, "Toward a Theology," 331.

69. Ann Ulanov and Barry Ulanov, *Primary Speech: A Psychology of Prayer* (Atlanta: John Knox Press, 1983), 63–72.

70. Virginia Ramey Mollenkott, *Godding: Human Responsibility and the Bible* (New York: Crossroad, 1987), 2. On "passion," see Carter Heyward, *Our Passion for Justice* (New York: Pilgrim Press, 1984), 19–23.

71. Beverly Wildung Harrison, *Making the Connections: Essays in Feminist Social Ethics,* ed. Carol S. Robb (Boston: Beacon Press, 1985), 14.

72. Elsa Tamez, *The Scandalous Message of James: Faith without Works Is Dead* (New York: Crossroad, 1990), 53.

73. I discuss these inconsistencies in more detail in Kathleen J. Greider, "Reckoning with Aggression: Investigations in Violence and Vitality," *Journal of Pastoral Theology* 6 (June 1996):37–54.

74. Catherine Mumford Booth, *Papers on Aggressive Christianity* (London: John Snow and Co., 1891), 11.

75. Ronald H. Rottschafer, "The Passive Christian: Personality Disorder or Role Play," *Journal of Psychology and Christianity* 3 (Spring 1984):42–51.

76. These dynamics are discussed in depth in chapter 4.

77. For this approach, see Harriet Goldhor Lerner, *Women in Therapy* (New York: Harper & Row, 1988).

78. See, for example, Teresa Bernardez-Bonesatti, "Women and Anger: Conflicts with Aggression in Contemporary Women," *Journal of the American Medical Women's Association* 33 (May 1978):215–19; Anne Campbell, *Men, Women, and Aggression* (New York: Basic Books, 1993).

79. Poling, *The Abuse of Power,* 106.

80. See, for example, Joel Kovel, *White Racism: A Psychohistory* (New York: Pantheon Books, 1970); Amos N. Wilson, *Black-on-Black Violence: The Psychodynamics of Black Self-Annihilation in Service of White Domination* (New York: Afrikan World Infosystems, 1990).

81. bell hooks, *Ain't I a Woman: Black Women and Feminism* (Boston: South End Press, 1981), 159–60.

82. Cited by hooks, 160.

83. Examples of this literature include Ada María Isasi-Díaz, *En la Lucha (In the Struggle): A Hispanic Women's Liberation Theology* (Minneapolis: Fortress Press, 1993); Chung Hyun Kyung, *Struggle to Be the Sun Again: Introducing Asian Women's Theology* (Maryknoll, N.Y.: Orbis Books, 1990); Robert Goss, *Jesus Acted Up: A Gay and Lesbian Manifesto* (San Francisco: HarperSanFrancisco, 1993).

84. Walter Wink calls this dynamic "the myth of redemptive violence" (*Engaging the Powers: Discernment and Resistance in a World of Domination* [Minneapolis: Fortress Press, 1992], 17–25).

85. Campbell, *Men, Women, and Aggression,* 179–80, n. 16.

86. Jean Baker Miller and Janet Surrey, "Revisioning Women's Anger: The Personal and

the Global," *Work in Progress* 43 (Wellesley, Mass.: The Stone Center Working Paper Series, 1990): 1.

Notes to Chapter 2.
What Is Aggression?

1. Erich Fromm, *The Anatomy of Human Destructiveness* (New York: Holt, Rinehart, & Winston, 1973), 3.
2. D. W. Winnicott, *Deprivation and Delinquency,* ed. Clare Winnicott, Ray Shepherd, and Madeleine Davis (New York: Tavistock Publishers, 1984), 92.
3. That an object relations theorist gives significant weight to drives may seem surprising or contradictory. See Jay R. Greenberg and Stephen A. Mitchell, *Object Relations in Psychoanalytic Theory* (Cambridge, Mass.: Harvard University Press, 1983),197–201. Winnicott's model remains solidly relational: relationship and environment play the central role in the development of the self. Further, he radically revises the concept of drives: drives are seen as only one factor, and not the primary one, in the development of the self and relationship. Additionally, the drives are relationally significant: drives are object-seeking, not simply pleasure-seeking. However, through his discussion of drives, the important and still little-understood relationship between physiology and emotion rightly retains a significant place in Winnicottian theory. In Winnicott's view, drives play a primary role in the building up "of the feeling that one's person is in one's body" (D. W. Winnicott, "Primitive Emotional Development," in *Through Paediatrics to Psychoanalysis,* ed. Masud R. Khan [New York: Basic Books, 1975], 150–51).
4. In animal studies, *instinct* refers to an innate, continuous compulsion to seek a particular goal. In general, human beings are shaped by a more complex relational environment and have greater capacity to moderate our response to stimuli on the basis of experience and reflection. Thus, the words *drive* and *impulse* generally are used to indicate the involuntary but nondeterminative pressure of human biology. Stephen Mitchell describes the difference this way: Drive is "a psycho-physiological reaction in a relational context," while instinct is more like an "extrapsychological push deriving from the body" (Mitchell, *Hope and Dread in Psychoanalysis* [New York: Basic Books, 1993], 165–66). To say that aggression is a drive is not to say that we have no choices about how we live out this powerful energy, but that we have no choice about whether to have it.
5. Winnicott, *Through Paediatrics,* 216.
6. Luigi Valzelli, *Psychobiology of Aggression and Violence* (New York: Raven Press, 1981), 27–28.
7. "Instinctual aggressiveness . . . is originally a part of appetite, or of some other form of instinctual love" (Winnicott, *Deprivation,* 87–88).
8. Winnicott is somewhat inconsistent on this point. He refers to the "original fusion of love and aggression" (*Deprivation,* 88). He also says that the fusion of love and aggression is an achievement of maturity: the child "has become able to combine erotic and aggressive experience" (*The Maturational Processes and the Facilitating Environment: Studies in the Theory of Emotional Development* [Madison, Conn.: International Universities Press, 1965], 75). I interpret Winnicott to be say-

ing that while love and aggression are never actually split, never without relationship, they often feel to us to be split. When under threat, the ability to retain *consciousness* of and act out of the close relationship between aggression and love is an achievement of maturity.

9. The explication of "life force" that follows is mine. The notion of a neutral or ambivalent life force is used by other psychoanalytic theorists but, to my knowledge, not developed by any of them. Interestingly, the majority of the theorists who support this more open-ended view of aggression are women: Karen Horney, *New Ways in Psychoanalysis* (New York: W. W. Norton, 1939); Phyllis Greenacre, *Emotional Growth: Psychoanalytic Studies of the Gifted and a Great Variety of Other Individuals,* vol. 1. (New York: International Universities Press, 1958), 113–27; Anthony Storr, *Human Aggression* (New York: Atheneum, 1968); Janine Chasseguet-Smirgel, "Feminine Guilt and the Oedipus Complex," in *Female Sexuality,* ed. J. Chasseguet-Smirgel (Ann Arbor: University of Michigan Press, 1970), 94–134; Henri Parens, *The Development of Aggression in Early Childhood* (New York: Aronson, 1979); Toni Bernay, "Reconciling Nurturance and Aggression: A New Feminine Identity," in *The Psychology of Today's Woman: New Psychoanalytic Visions,* ed. Toni Bernay and Dorothy W. Cantor (Cambridge, Mass.: Harvard University Press, 1989); Dorothy W. Cantor and Toni Bernay, with Jean Stoess, *Women in Power: The Secrets of Leadership* (Boston: Houghton-Mifflin Co., 1992).

10. It would be naive to define *aggression* as an expression of power of the life force without quickly acknowledging that we often express our life force in ways that do intentional as well as unintentional harm to the life force manifested in others. We will attend to this reality later in the chapter.

11. Adelbert H. Jenkins, *The Psychology of the Afro-American: A Humanistic Approach* (New York: Pergamon Press, 1982), 159. Though often included as part of basic aggressiveness, I have intentionally not included the more oppositional notions of mastery or competition. They can be a part of aggression, even constructively. But opposition is not part of the essential meaning of aggression, in my view.

12. "Drives constitute a hierarchically supraordinate motivational system comprising affects that are their building blocks" (Otto F. Kernberg, "The Psychopathology of Hatred," in *Rage, Power, and Aggression,* ed. Robert A. Glick and Steven P. Roose [New Haven, Conn.: Yale University Press, 1993], 61).

13. Daniel N. Stern, *The Interpersonal World of the Infant: A View from Psychoanalysis and Developmental Psychology* (New York: Basic Books, 1985), 54–61.

14. Ibid., 56.

15. Ibid., 54. Stern does not discuss the relationship between aggression and vitality affects, but these descriptive words parallel notions of aggressiveness.

16. Winnicott, *Through Paediatrics,* 204.

17. Winnicott, *Deprivation,* 93.

18. Edrita Fried, *Active/Passive: The Crucial Psychological Dimension* (New York: Grune & Stratton, 1970), 3–23.

19. Karen Horney, *Neurosis and Human Growth: The Struggle Toward Self-Realization* (New York: W. W. Norton and Co., 1950), 19.

20. Jean Baker Miller and Janet Surrey, "Revisioning Women's Anger: The Personal and

the Global," *Work in Progress* 43 (Wellesley, Mass.: The Stone Center Working Paper Series, 1990), 2.

21. Winnicott, *Through Paediatrics,* 243–54.

22. Organic causes of unprovoked violence include head trauma, neurological damage secondary to use of alcohol and drugs of abuse, reactions to prescribed medications, anoxia and hypoxemia, electrolyte disturbances, endocrine disorders, genetic and developmental disorders, epilepsy, the dyscontrol syndrome, space-occupying lesions, infections, dementias, cerebral vascular disease, and the biological components of some mental illnesses (affective disorders such as mania or depression, schizophrenia, and character disorders, especially antisocial personality disorder). See Dennis J. Kutzer, "Psychobiological Factors in Violent Behavior," in *Assessment and Intervention,* vol. 1: *Violent Behavior,* ed. Leonard J. Hertzberg, Gene F. Ostrum, and Joan Roberts Field (Great Neck, N.Y.: PMA Publishing Co., 1990), 29–40.

23. Winnicott focused on the relationship between mother and child. I use terms that suggest a wider spectrum of loving presences around the child—parents, extended family, close friends, and teachers.

24. Winnicott, *Through Paediatrics,* 300–305. Winnicott refers to this period as primary *maternal* preoccupation. He emphasizes the mother because of the physical familiarity between mother and child. Their unique physical bond deepens after birth if the baby is nursed. Though Winnicott makes an important point, I prefer to call this period simply "primary preoccupation" to underline that, despite the unique physical relationship between mother and child, others can and must provide this support to the baby. The revision is also appropriate in light of changing social roles. Winnicott's ideas can be helpfully extended to fathers and close others.

25. Margaret S. Mahler, Fred Pine, and Anni Bergman, *The Psychological Birth of the Human Infant: Symbiosis and Individuation* (New York: Basic Books, 1975).

26. Winnicott, *Maturational Processes,* 31–32.

27. Winnicott, *Through Paediatrics,* 303.

28. Ibid., 304.

29. Winnicott, *Deprivation,* 98–99.

30. Winnicott, *Maturational Processes,* 180.

31. Winnicott, *Through Paediatrics,* 211.

32. Ibid., 210.

33. Ibid., 206.

34. Ibid., 216.

35. See, for example, W.R.D. Fairbairn, *Psychoanalytic Studies of the Personality* (London: Routledge, 1994).

36. Winnicott, *Through Paediatrics,* 206.

37. Marshall H. Segall, "Aggression in Global Perspective: A Research Strategy," in *Aggression in Global Perspective,* ed. Arnold P. Goldstein and Marshall H. Segall (New York: Pergamon Press, 1983), 28–30.

38. Winnicott, *Deprivation,* 227.

39. D. W. Winnicott, *Playing and Reality* (London: Tavistock Publications, 1971), 93.

40. Winnicott, *Maturational Processes,* 145–46.

41. If the failures are traumatic—too intense or prolonged—they play a role in the emergence of violence, the issue we take up in the next section.

42. Winnicott, *Through Paediatrics,* 214–18.

43. Winnicott, *Deprivation*, 115.

44. Racial and gender awareness are normally in place by the age of two or three. See Thomas A. Parham, *Psychological Storms: The African American Struggle for Identity* (Chicago: African American Images, 1993), 78; Anne Campbell, *Men, Women, and Aggression* (New York: Basic Books, 1993), 25–26.

45. Parham, *Psychological Storms*.

46. Winnicott, *Deprivation*, 115.

47. Greenberg and Mitchell, *Object Relations*, 159–60.

48. Winnicott, *Deprivation*, 115.

49. Winnicott, *Playing*, 89.

50. Winnicott, *Deprivation*, 100–105.

51. Melanie Klein, "Love, Guilt and Reparation," in *Love, Guilt and Reparation and Other Works 1921–1945*, vol. 1: *The Writings of Melanie Klein* (New York: Free Press, 1975).

52. Winnicott, *Playing*, 93.

53. Ibid., 90.

54. Ibid., 93.

55. The concept of the facilitating environment is developed throughout Winnicott, *Maturational Processes*.

56. Winnicott, *Playing*, 2.

57. Space does not allow the full development of these fascinating concepts. See Winnicott, *Playing*, 1–25.

58. Winnicott, *Through Paediatrics*, 217.

59. Winnicott, *Maturational Processes*, 148.

60. Winnicott, *Through Paediatrics*, 214.

61. Winnicott, *Playing*, 70.

62. Winnicott, *Maturational Processes*, 145–50.

63. Judith V. Jordan, Alexandra G. Kaplan, Jean Baker Miller et al., *Women's Growth in Connection: Writings from the Stone Center* (New York: Guilford Press, 1991), 17–20.

64. Winnicott, *Deprivation*, 100–105, 136–44.

65. Campbell, *Men, Women, and Aggression*, 15–16.

66. Albert Bandura, *Aggression: A Social Learning Analysis* (Englewood Cliffs, N.J.: Prentice-Hall, 1973).

67. The implications of this are intriguing in terms of the social representations of aggression appropriate according to socially constructed categories of gender and race. We explore this further in chapter 4.

68. Jane Flax, *Thinking Fragments: Psychoanalysis, Feminism, and Postmodernism in the Contemporary West* (Berkeley: University of California Press, 1990), 119.

69. Karen Horney tells us that "doubts" about two aspects of Freudian theory led ultimately to her revision of psychoanalysis; interestingly, those two issues were aggression and gender. Karen Horney, *New Ways in Psychoanalysis* (New York: W. W. Norton, 1939), 7.

70. Karen Horney, "Human Nature Can Change," *American Journal of Psychoanalysis* 12 (1952): 68.

71. Fromm, *The Anatomy of Destructiveness*.

72. Richard B. Felson and James T. Tedeschi, eds., *Aggression and Violence: Social Interactionist Perspectives* (Washington, D.C.: American Psychological Association, 1993), 1–2.

73. Winnicott, *Deprivation,* 91.
74. D. W. Winnicott, *Babies and Their Mothers,* ed. Clare Winnicott, Ray Shepherd, and Madeleine Davis (Reading, Mass.: Addison-Wesley Publishing Co., 1987), 8.
75. Alice Miller, *The Drama of the Gifted Child: The Search for the True Self,* trans. Ruth Ward (New York: Basic Books, 1981), 64–76.
76. Miller, *Drama,* 69.
77. Winnicott, *Through Paediatrics,* 208.
78. Winnicott, *Deprivation,* 176.
79. Ibid., 225.
80. Winnicott, *Through Paediatrics,* 204.
81. Winnicott, *Deprivation,* 195.
82. Ibid.
83. Winnicott, *Deprivation,* 245–46.
84. Winnicott, *Through Paediatrics,* 213.
85. Ibid., 314.
86. Carol Gilligan, *In a Different Voice: Psychological Theory and Women's Development* (Cambridge, Mass.: Harvard University Press, 1982), 173.
87. Harry Guntrip, *Schizoid Phenomena, Object Relations, and the Self* (New York: International Universities Press, 1969), 26.
88. James W. Prescott, "Affectional Bonding for the Prevention of Violent Behaviors: Neurobiological, Psychological and Religious/Spiritual Determinants," in *Assessment and Intervention,* vol. 1: *Violent Behavior,* ed. Leonard J. Hertzberg, Gene F. Ostrum, and Joan Roberts Field (Great Neck, N.Y.: PMA Publishing Co., 1990).
89. Winnicott, *Deprivation,* 110.
90. Winnicott, *Through Paediatrics,* 303.
91. Ibid., 217.
92. Guntrip, *Schizoid Phenomena,* 172.
93. Heinz Kohut, *The Analysis of the Self: A Systematic Approach to the Psychoanalytic Treatment of Narcissistic Personality Disorders* (Madison, Conn.: International Universities Press, 1971), 25–34.
94. Ibid.
95. Heinz Kohut, "Thoughts on Narcissism and Narcissistic Rage," in *The Search for the Self: Selected Writings of Heinz Kohut,* ed. Paul Ornstein (New York: International Universities Press, 1978), 615–36.
96. Heinz Kohut, *The Restoration of the Self* (Madison, Conn.: International Universities Press, 1977), 114.
97. Heinz Kohut, "Thoughts on Narcissism," 636–58.

Notes to Chapter 3.
Toward a Theology of Aggression

1. W. W. Meissner, "Toward a Theology of Human Aggression," *Journal of Religion and Health* 10 (October 1971): 325.
2. Ibid., 324.
3. Ibid., 332.

4. Kyle A. Pasewark, *A Theology of Power: Being beyond Domination* (Minneapolis: Fortress Press, 1993), 1.

5. Chris M. Meadows, "A Constructive View of Anger, Aggression, and Violence," *Pastoral Psychology* 22 (September 1971): 14.

6. Ibid.

7. Rosemary Radford Ruether, *Gaia and God: An Ecofeminist Theology of Earth Healing* (San Francisco: HarperSanFrancisco, 1992), 26–27.

8. Kathleen M. Sands, *Escape from Paradise: Evil and Tragedy in Feminist Theology* (Minneapolis: Fortress Press, 1994), 10.

9. Ibid., 13.

10. I. Carter Heyward, *The Redemption of God: A Theology of Mutual Relation* (Lanham, Md.: University Press of America, 1982), 151.

11. Sands, an allusion to the title of her book, *Escape from Paradise*.

12. Douglas John Hall, *Imaging God: Dominion as Stewardship* (Grand Rapids: Wm. B. Eerdmans Publishing Co., 1986).

13. Ibid., 116.

14. Ibid., 123–24

15. Ibid., 113–23.

16. Ibid., 118.

17. Ibid., 186.

18. Other frameworks for naming distorted and unethical forms of power bear some resemblance to my focus on violence, lack of vitality/passivity, and vitality: for example, power-over and power-under, in Mary Parker Follett, *Creative Experience* (New York: Longmans, Green, 1924) and Follett, *Dynamic Administration* (New York, Harper & Brothers, 1942); overpowered or overpowering, underpowered, and empowered, in Carrie Doehring, *Taking Care: Monitoring Power Dynamics and Relational Boundaries in Pastoral Care and Counseling* (Nashville: Abingdon, 1995); undivided and shared power, in Dorothee Soelle, *Of War and Love,* trans. Rita Kimber and Robert Kimber (Maryknoll, N.Y.: Orbis Books, 1983).

19. Dorothee Soelle and Fulbert Steffensky, *Not Just Yes and Amen* (Philadelphia: Fortress Press, 1985), 16–17.

20. Eileen A. Gavin, "Words Can Never Hurt Me? The Psychological/Emotional Abuse of Children," in *Clinical Handbook of Pastoral Counseling*, vol. 2, ed. Robert J. Wicks and Richard D. Parsons (New York: Paulist Press, Integration Books, 1993), 507.

21. Ibid., 507–11.

22. Dorothee Soelle, *Choosing Life,* trans. Margaret Kohh (Philadelphia: Fortress Press, 1981), 35.

23. Carter Heyward, *Touching Our Strength: The Erotic as Power and the Love of God* (San Francisco: Harper & Row, 1989), 55.

24. Soelle and Steffensky, *Not Just Yes,* 16.

25. Marjorie Hewitt Suchocki, *The Fall to Violence: Original Sin in Relational Theology* (New York: Continuum, 1994), 85.

26. Dorothee Soelle, *The Arms Race Kills Even without War,* trans. Gerhard A. Elston (Philadelphia: Fortress Press, 1983), 89.

27. Heyward, *Redemption,* 154.

28. Soelle finds a theological root of such states of being in images of God being dis-

passionate, "above it all": "When a being who is free from suffering is worshipped as God, then it is possible to train oneself in patience, endurance, imperturbability, and aloofness from suffering" (*Suffering,* trans. Everett R. Kalin [Philadelphia: Fortress Press, 1975], 43).

29. Carter Heyward, *Our Passion for Justice: Images of Power, Sexuality, and Liberation* (New York: Beacon Press, 1984), 123–31.

30. Heyward, *Redemption,* 155.

31. Soelle, *Choosing Life,* 69.

32. Heyward, *Redemption,* 164–65.

33. Heyward, *Passion,* 20.

34. Edward Farley, *Good and Evil: Interpreting a Human Condition* (Minneapolis: Fortress Press, 1990), 180.

35. Ibid., 146.

36. Ibid., 181.

37. Ibid.

38. Ibid., 181–82.

39. Howard Clinebell, *Counseling for Spiritually Empowered Wholeness: A Hope-Centered Approach* (New York: Haworth Pastoral Press, 1995), 28.

40. Ibid., 30.

41. Rita Nakashima Brock, *Journeys by Heart: A Christology of Erotic Power* (New York: Crossroad, 1991), xiv.

42. John Macmurray, *Persons in Relation* (New York: Harper & Brothers, 1961), 118.

43. Starhawk, *Truth or Dare: Encounters with Power, Authority, and Mystery* (San Francisco: Harper & Row, 1987), 10.

44. Heyward, *Redemption,* 54.

45. Heyward, *Touching Our Strength,* 93.

46. Meissner, "Toward a Theology," 325.

47. The centrality of resistance to authentic Christian life is also argued in the following: James Newton Poling, *Deliver Us from Evil: Resisting Racial and Gender Oppression* (Minneapolis: Fortress Press, 1996); Christine M. Smith, *Preaching as Weeping, Confession, and Resistance: Radical Responses to Radical Evil* (Louisville, Ky.: Westminster/John Knox Press, 1992); Sharon D. Welch, *Communities of Resistance and Solidarity: A Feminist Theology of Liberation* (Maryknoll, N.Y.: Orbis Books, 1985).

48. Welch, *Communities of Resistance,* 4.

49. Patricia Hill Collins, *Black Feminist Thought: Knowledge, Consciousness, and the Politics of Empowerment* (New York: Routledge & Kegan Paul, 1991).

50. Poling, *Deliver Us from Evil,* 104.

51. Collins, *Black Feminist Thought,* 182.

52. Ibid., 18.

53. Ibid., 44.

54. Welch, *Communities of Resistance,* 78–80.

55. Poling, *Deliver Us from Evil,* 106.

56. Ibid., 107.

57. Collins, *Black Feminist Thought,* 92, 103–13.

58. Mary Field Belenky, Blythe McVicker Clinchy, Nancy Rule Goldberger, Jill Mattuck Tarule, *Women's Ways of Knowing: The Development of Self, Voice, and Mind* (New York: Basic Books, 1986), 23–34.

59. bell hooks, *Talking Back: Thinking Feminist, Thinking Black* (Boston: South End Press, 1989), 5–9.

60. Smith, *Preaching as Weeping,* 5.

61. Johann Baptist Metz, *Faith and History in Society: Toward a Practical Fundamental Theology* (New York: Seabury Press, 1980), 66–67. Cited by Welch, *Communities of Resistance,* 36.

62. Smith, *Preaching as Weeping,* 6.

63. Ibid., 5.

64. Collins, *Black Feminist Thought,* 141.

65. Ibid., 91.

66. Smith, *Preaching as Weeping,* 5.

67. Poling, *Deliver Us from Evil,* xi–xii.

68. Dorothee Soelle, *Death by Bread Alone,* trans. David L. Scheidt (Philadelphia: Fortress Press, 1978), 98–99.

69. Martin Luther King, Jr., "The Power of Nonviolence," in *A Testament of Hope: The Essential Writings and Speeches of Martin Luther King, Jr.,* ed. James M. Washington (San Francisco: HarperCollins, 1986), 7.

70. M. K. Gandhi, *Non-Violent Resistance (Satyagraha)* (New York: Schocken Books, 1961), 38.

71. Ibid., 176.

72. Ibid., 36, emphasis added.

73. Martin Luther King, Jr., "The Most Durable Power," in *A Testament of Hope,* 10–11.

74. Martin Luther King, Jr., "An Experiment in Love," in *A Testament of Hope,* 17.

75. Walter Wink, *Engaging the Powers: Discernment and Resistance in a World of Domination* (Minneapolis: Fortress Press, 1992), 294.

76. Martin Luther King, Jr., "Nonviolence and Racial Justice," in *A Testament of Hope,* 7–8.

77. Mark Juergensmeyer, *Fighting with Gandhi* (San Francisco: Harper & Row, 1984), 151–55.

78. Martin Luther King, Jr., "Pilgrimage to Nonviolence," in *A Testament of Hope,"* 39.

79. Martin Luther King, Jr., "The Case Against Tokenism," in *A Testament of Hope*, 108. For discussion of this concept, see Garth Baker-Fletcher, *Somebodyness: Martin Luther King, Jr., and the Theory of Dignity* (Minneapolis: Fortress Press, 1993).

80. King, "The Most Durable Power," 10.

81. King, "The Power of Nonviolence," 15.

82. Martin Luther King, Jr., "The Strength to Love," in *A Testament of Hope,* 494–97.

83. Gandhi, *Non-Violent Resistance,* iv.

84. King, "Nonviolence and Racial Justice," 8.

85. Wink, *Engaging the Powers,* 289–90.

86. Dorothy Parker, excerpt from "The Veteran," *The Portable Dorothy Parker,* rev. and enlarged ed. (New York: Viking Penguin, 1973), 101. Copyright 1926, renewed 1954 by Dorothy Parker. Used by permission of Viking Penguin, a division of Penguin Books USA Inc.

87. Some violence may be in defense of life and, therefore, necessary. Nonviolence may not be sufficient for everyone just because it is sufficient for some. Condemnation of all forms of violent revolution may be steeped in racial and/or class privilege. See The Amanecida Collective, *Revolutionary Forgiveness: Feminist Reflections on Nicaragua,* ed. Anne Gilson and Carter Heyward (Maryknoll, N.Y.: Orbis Books, 1987), 69. It is often steeped in gender privilege as well.

88. Mercy Amba Oduyoye, "Be a Woman, and Africa Will Be Strong," in *Inheriting Our Mother's Gardens: Feminist Theology in Third World Perspective,* ed. Letty M. Russell, Kwok Pui-Lan, Ada María Isasi-Díaz, Katie Geneva Cannon (Philadelphia: Westminster Press, 1988), 35.

Notes to Chapter 4. Aggression in Cultural Context:
Gender, Race, Oppression

1. See David W. Augsburger, *Conflict Mediation across Cultures: Pathways and Patterns* (Louisville, Ky.: Westminster/John Knox Press, 1992); Arnold P. Goldstein and Marshall H. Segall, eds., *Aggression in Global Perspective* (New York: Pergamon Press, 1983); David Levinson, *Family Violence in Cross-Cultural Perspective* (Newbury Park, Calif.: Sage Publications, 1989); David Levinson, *Aggression and Conflict: A Cross-Cultural Encyclopedia* (Santa Barbara, Calif.: ABC-CLIO, 1994). In contrast, cultural differences in constructive aggressiveness—initiative, assertion, boldness, and the like—are rarely addressed, despite the fact that differences in assertion are frequently precipitants to aggressive conflicts.
2. In naming race and gender as cultures, I am following the definition of Elaine Pinderhughes: "Culture may be defined as the sum total of ways of living developed by a group of human beings to meet biological and psychosocial needs" (*Understanding Race, Ethnicity and Power: The Key to Efficacy in Clinical Practice* [New York: Free Press, 1989], 6). Also central to my argument is the view that culture "is not explicitly taught nor is it effortlessly learned. Rather it is absorbed in the process of socialization and strengthened and amplified in the course of lifelong incidental learnings" (Juris G. Draguns, "Dilemmas and Choices in Cross-Cultural Counseling: The Universal versus the Culturally Distinctive," in *Counseling across Cultures,* 3d ed., ed. Paul B. Pedersen, Juris G. Draguns, Walter J. Lonner, and Joseph E. Trimble [Honolulu: University of Hawaii Press, 1989], 3).
3. Anne Campbell, *Men, Women, and Aggression* (New York: Basic Books, 1993).
4. Ibid., 1.
5. Ibid., 2–7.
6. Ibid., 72. Campbell argues that scientists' theories about aggression can be similarly divided (pp. 7–14). These two ways of understanding aggression's meanings also loosely parallel the two purposes of aggression identified by Winnicott—an expression of the life force and a means of responding to threat—though his understandings leave more room for potentially positive meanings.
7. Ibid., 20.
8. Ibid., 19.
9. J. Langlois and A. Downes, "Mothers and Peers as Socialization Agents of Sex-Typed Play Behaviors in Young Children," Psychology Department, University of Texas, Austin, 1979. Cited by Campbell, *Men, Women, and Aggression,* 21.
10. M. E. Snow, C. N. Jacklin, and E. E. Maccoby, "Sex of Child Differences in Father-Child Interaction at One Year," *Child Development* 54 (1983):227–32. Cited by Campbell, *Men, Women, and Aggression,* 21.
11. Campbell, *Men, Women, and Aggression,* 25.

12. B. I. Fagot, M. D. Leinbach, and R. Hagan, "Gender Labeling and the Development of Sex-Typed Behaviors," *Developmental Psychology* 22 (1986):440–43. Cited by Campbell, *Men, Women, and Aggression,* 26.
13. Campbell, *Men, Women, and Aggression,* 26.
14. Ibid.
15. B. I. Fagot, "Beyond the Reinforcement Principle: Another Step Toward an Understanding of Sex Role Development," *Developmental Psychology* 21 (1985): 1097–1104. Cited by Campbell, *Men, Women, and Aggression,* 31.
16. Campbell, *Men, Women, and Aggression,* 30.
17. Ibid.
18. Ibid., 27.
19. Ibid., 28.
20. Ibid., 27.
21. Ibid., 20.
22. Janet L. Surrey, "The Relational Self in Women: Clinical Implications," in *Women's Growth in Connection: Writings from the Stone Center,* ed. Judith V. Jordan, Alexandra G. Kaplan, Jean Baker Miller et al. (New York: Guilford Press, 1991), 38.
23. Campbell, *Men, Women, and Aggression,* 27.
24. Ibid., 20.
25. Ibid., 33.
26. Ibid., 32.
27. Ibid., 30.
28. Ibid., 34–35.
29. Ibid., 69–85.
30. Ibid., 1.
31. Deborah Tannen, *You Just Don't Understand: Men and Women in Conversation* (New York: Ballantine Books, 1990). See especially her discussion of gender differences in styles of conflict, pp. 149–87.
32. Carol Gilligan, *In a Different Voice: Psychological Theory and Women's Development* (Cambridge, Mass.: Harvard University Press, 1982), 42.
33. Campbell, *Men, Women, and Aggression,* 2.
34. Ibid., 142.
35. Audre Lorde, *Sister Outsider: Essays and Speeches* (Trumansburg, N.Y.: Crossing Press, 1984), 74.
36. Ibid., 76.
37. Ibid., 77.
38. Charles A. Pinderhughes, "Identification and Aggression Issues in Racial Integration and Racial Unification," in *Psychoanalytic Perspectives on Aggression,* ed. George D. Goldman and Donald S. Milman (Dubuque, Iowa: Kendall/Hunt Publishing Co., 1978), 54.
39. Gordon W. Allport, *The Nature of Prejudice* (Boston: Beacon Press, 1954).
40. Alexander Thomas and Samuel Sillen, *Racism and Psychiatry* (Secaucus, N.J.: Citadel Press, 1972), 112–13.
41. Emilie M. Townes, *In a Blaze of Glory: Womanist Spirituality as Social Witness* (Nashville: Abingdon Press, 1995), 50.
42. U.S. Bureau of the Census, 1993 Report, data obtained through the Internet.

43. U.S. Bureau of the Census, *Poverty in the United States: 1992* (Washington, D.C.: U.S. Government Printing Office, 1993). Cited by Heather E. Bullock, "Class Acts: Middle-Class Responses to the Poor," in *The Social Psychology of Interpersonal Discrimination,* ed. Bernice Lott and Diane Malluso (New York: Guilford Press, 1995), 123.

44. C. Gorman, "Why Do Blacks Die Young?" *Time,* 16 September 1991, 50–52. Cited by Bullock, "Class Acts," 136–37.

45. Robert D. Bullard and Beverly H. Wright, "Toxic Waste and the African American Community," in *Prescriptions and Policies: The Social Well-Being of African Americans in the 1990's,* ed. Dionne J. Jones (New Brunswick, N.J.: Transaction Publishers, 1991), 67–68. Cited by Townes, *In a Blaze of Glory,* 55.

46. Townes, *In a Blaze of Glory,* 47–67.

47. Na'im Akbar, *Chains and Images of Psychological Slavery* (Jersey City, N.J.: New Mind Productions, 1984).

48. Ibid., 42.

49. Ibid., 43–44.

50. Ibid., 44.

51. Ibid., 43.

52. "The European world is on the verge of self-destruction. . . . It has gotten somehow consumed by its own consumption . . . [and] cannot naturally correct its addiction to excess" (Ibid., 44–45).

53. Ibid., 52–55.

54. Ibid., 52.

55. C. Pierce, "Offensive Mechanisms," in *The Black Seventies,* ed. F. Barbour (Boston: Sargent Publishers, 1970). Cited by E. Pinderhughes, *Understanding Race,* 84.

56. E. Pinderhughes, *Understanding Race,* 84.

57. Akbar, *Chains and Images,* 1.

58. Ibid., 2.

59. Ibid., 34.

60. Amos Wilson, *Black-on-Black Violence: The Psychodynamics of Black Self-Annihilation in Service of White Domination* (New York: Afrikan World Infosystems, 1990). I am grateful to Garth Baker-Fletcher for bringing Wilson's work to my attention.

61. Anna Freud, *The Ego and the Mechanisms of Defense,* rev. ed., vol. 2: *The Writings of Anna Freud* (New York: International Universities Press, 1966), 109–21.

62. Ibid., 113.

63. Sigmund Freud, *Beyond the Pleasure Principle,* vol. 18: *The Standard Edition of the Complete Psychological Works of Freud,* trans. James Strachey (London: Hogarth, 1953–74), 17. Cited by A. Freud, *The Ego,* 113.

64. Wilson, *Black-on-Black Violence,* 105–22.

65. Ibid., 108.

66. Ibid.

67. Ibid., 114–15.

68. I discuss these issues more fully in Kathleen J. Greider, "Too Militant? Aggression, Gender, and the Construction of Justice," in *Through the Eyes of Women: Insights for Pastoral Care,* ed. Jeanne Stevenson Moessner (Minneapolis: Fortress Press, 1996).

69. Joel Kovel, *White Racism: A Psychohistory* (New York: Pantheon Books, 1970), 32.
70. Thistlethwaite, 146 n. 9. Thistlethwaite notes that she has adapted Mary Pellauer's notion of "recovering sexist." Mary Pellauer in an address at Lutheran School of Theology, October 1987. Cited by Susan B. Thistlethwaite, *Sex, Race, and God: Christian Feminism in Black and White* (New York: Crossroad, 1989), 162 n.10.
71. Ibid., 12, 146 n.9.
72. Carrie Doehring, *Taking Care: Monitoring Power Dynamics and Relational Boundaries in Pastoral Care and Counseling* (Nashville: Abingdon Press, 1995), 57.
73. Lorde, *Sister Outsider,* 125.
74. Ibid., 130.
75. Nicolina M. Fedele and Elizabeth A. Harrington, "Women's Groups: How Connections Heal," *Work in Progress* (Wellesley, Mass.: Stone Center Working Paper Series, 1990).
76. Janet L. Surrey, "Relationship and Empowerment," in *Women's Growth in Connection: Writings from the Stone Center,* ed. Judith V. Jordan, Alexandra G. Kaplan, Jean Baker Miller et al. (New York: Guilford Press, 1991).
77. Cheryl Townsend Gilkes, "The Black Church as a Therapeutic Community: Suggested Areas for Research into the Black Religious Experience," *Journal of the Interdenominational Theological Center* 8 (Fall 1980): 29–44.
78. Thomas A. Parham, *Psychological Storms: The African American Struggle for Identity* (Chicago: African American Images, 1993), 65–80.
79. For a discussion of the discriminatory use of aggressive stereotypes, see the discussion of racism in society's response to African American women who kill their abusers, in Lenore E. Walker, *Terrifying Love: Why Battered Women Kill and How Society Responds* (New York: HarperPerennial, 1989), 206–18.
80. See, for example, bell hooks, *Killing Rage: Ending Racism* (New York: Henry Holt and Co., 1995); Ellis Cose, *The Rage of a Privileged Class* (New York: HarperPerennial, 1993); Mary Valentis and Anne Devane, *Female Rage: Unlocking Its Secrets, Claiming Its Power* (New York: Carol Southern Books, 1994).
81. Dorothee Soelle, *Suffering,* trans. Everett R. Kalin (Philadelphia: Fortress Press, 1975), 70.
82. Jean Baker Miller, "The Necessity of Conflict," in *Women Changing Therapy: New Assessments, Values and Strategies in Feminist Therapy,* ed. Joan Hamerman Robbins and Rachel Josefowitz Siegel (New York: Harrington Park Press, 1985).
83. Lorde, *Sister Outsider,* 128.
84. Cheryl J. Sanders, "Black Women in Biblical Perspective: Resistance, Affirmation, and Empowerment," in *Living the Intersection: Womanism and Afrocentrism in Theology,* ed. Cheryl J. Sanders (Minneapolis: Fortress Press, 1995), 130, 138.
85. Timothy Williams, "We Need More Like Granny Lewis," *Los Angeles Times,* 5 March 1995, B18.

Notes to Chapter 5.
Caring for Aggression

1. Marie M. Fortune and James Poling, "Calling to Accountability: The Church's Response to Abusers," in *Clinical Handbook of Pastoral Counseling,* vol. 2, ed. Robert J. Wicks and Richard D. Parsons (New York: Paulist Press, 1993), 492.

3. Marie M. Fortune, *Is Nothing Sacred?: When Sex Invades the Pastoral Relationship* (San Francisco: Harper & Row, Publishers, 1989), 130–33.

4. Thomas Moore, *Care of the Soul: A Guide for Cultivating Depth and Sacredness in Everyday Life* (New York: HarperCollins Publishers, 1992), 134.

5. Douglas L. Peterson, "Empathic Spiritual Direction," *Journal of Supervision and Training in Ministry* 5 (1982): 163.

6. Ann Ulanov and Barry Ulanov, *Primary Speech: A Psychology of Prayer* (Atlanta: John Knox Press, 1983), 63–64.

7. Ibid., 63.

8. Bill W., *Twelve Steps and Twelve Traditions* (New York: Alcoholics Anonymous Publishing, 1953).

9. Ulanov and Ulanov, *Primary Speech,* 67.

10. The autobiography of Andrew Young provides a window into a life lived with a powerfully positive blending of prayer and aggression. See Andrew Young, *A Way Out of No Way: The Spiritual Memoirs of Andrew Young* (Nashville: Thomas Nelson Publishers, 1994).

11. Ulanov and Ulanov, *Primary Speech,* 70.

12. Frank Deford, "The Women of Atlanta," *Newsweek,* 10 June 1996, 62–71, see esp. page 66.

13. For a helpful guide to speaking up, see Carolyn Stahl Bohler, *When You Need to Take a Stand* (Louisville, Ky.: Westminster/John Knox Press, 1990).

14. Andrew Sung Park, *The Wounded Heart of God: The Asian Concept of Han and the Christian Doctrine of Sin* (Nashville: Abingdon Press, 1993), 171.

15. Martin Luther King, Jr., "The Strength to Love," in *A Testament of Hope: The Essential Writings and Speeches of Martin Luther King, Jr.,* ed. James M. Washington (San Francisco: HarperCollins, 1986), 491–97.

16. Donald P. McNeill, Douglas A. Morrison, and Henri J. M. Nouwen, *Compassion: A Reflection on the Christian Life* (Garden City, N.Y.: Image Books, 1983), 125–26. Nouwen explores a related notion in his discussion of "movement from hostility to hospitality" in *Reaching Out: The Three Movements of the Spiritual Life* (New York: Image Books, 1975), 65–109.

17. McNeill, Morrison, and Nouwen, *Compassion,* 125.

18. Two excellent pastoral theological studies of anger are Andrew D. Lester, *Coping with Your Anger: A Christian Guide* (Philadelphia: Westminster Press, 1983) and Carroll Saussy, *The Gift of Anger: A Call to Faithful Action* (Louisville, Ky.: Westminster John Knox Press, 1995). For an equally helpful family systems approach, see Harriet Goldhor Lerner, *The Dance of Anger: A Woman's Guide to Changing the Patterns of Intimate Relationships* (New York: Harper & Row, 1985). Though Lerner's book was written with women especially in mind, it is also a valuable guide for men.

19. James D. Whitehead and Evelyn Eaton Whitehead, *Method in Ministry: Theological Reflection and Christian Ministry* (San Francisco: HarperSanFrancisco, 1980), 93–94.

20. Ibid., 93.

21. Ibid.

22. Ibid., 94.

Index

abuse/abusers. *See* trauma
action/active, 4, 17, 18, 22,
    24–25, 32, 35, 36, 46, 48, 59,
    63, 66, 68, 70, 71, 74, 83, 88,
    89, 91, 97, 99, 101–3, 105,
    107,,109, 110, 116, 117, 118
activism, 19, 70, 101–3, 116
African American(s), 30, 43,
    67–68, 79, 86–87, 87–103,
    110
aggression/aggressiveness. *See
    also* passive aggression;
    passivity/lack of vitality;
    violence; violent aggression;
    vitality
  ambiguity and relationality of,
    1–2, 5, 6, 13, 16–22, 30,
    32–55, 60–76, 81, 83–86, 92,
    95–96, 97–103, 104–19, 120
  and children, 33–35, 80–87
  and empathy, 50, 54, 55, 98,
    118
  and love, 5, 16, 26, 34–35,
    59–60, 118, 120, 128 nn.7, 8
  and play, 35, 42, 46–48 (as
    "potential space"), 54,
    81–82, 83, 84, 112–13, 115
  and the body, 25–26, 33–37,
    115–16
  and the sense of omnipotence,
    39, 46, 54, 109, 112
  as "almost synonymous with"
    movement, 34, 35–36
  as life-force and its defense,
    35, 21, 48–55, 75–76, 116,
    129 n.9, 135 n.87
  as reparation, 45, 47, 70, 96,
    97, 111, 114, 116
  building relationship to/with,
    6, 9, 40–41, 70, 71–72, 92,
    96, 107, 108, 108–16
  conflicts over expression of,
    106–7, 117
  definitions of, 1–2, 5, 8–9,
    21–22, 23–26, 32, 80
  gendering of, 2, 14, 15, 16, 22,
    29–31, 43, 77–79, 80–87,
    94–95, 96–97, 97–103
  healing/transformation of,
    104–19. *See also* healthy ag-
    gression; spirituality
  indirect vs. direct, 24–25
  insufficiency of theological re-
    flection on, 27–28, 56
  multivalency, 7, 9, 33, 58,
    74–75, 104
  origins of, 33–36, 48–55,
    57–60, 67–73, 80–97. *See
    also* violent aggression, ori-
    gins of
  politics of, 29, 78, 79
racialization of, 2–3, 5, 6, 8, 16,